LIVING STORIES
OF FAMOUS HYMNS

Living Stories
of Famous Hymns

by

ERNEST K. EMURIAN

Author of

Dramatized Stories of Hymns and Hymn Writers
More Dramatized Stories of Hymns and Hymn Writers
Plays and Pageants for Many Occasions
More Plays and Pageants for Many Occasions

Boston　W. A. WILDE COMPANY PUBLISHERS　Massachusetts

To
MARGARET
with love

PREFACE

LIVING STORIES OF FAMOUS HYMNS began as a newspaper column, HYMN OF THE WEEK, and was prepared with the encouragement and assistance of Robert Lewis and George Naylor, volunteer office secretaries of the Church, and editor and printer respectively of our monthly newsletter, THE ELM AVENEWS. With their cooperation, the column has appeared in many newspapers in the eastern seaboard states. I am grateful to them as well as to others of our Church's volunteer secretarial staff, for assisting me in the preparation of this book.

A word of appreciation is always due a congregation for permitting a minister to take the time necessary to produce a volume of this kind, and I am grateful to my wonderful people for affording me this privilege.

ERNEST K. EMURIAN
Elm Avenue Methodist Church, Portsmouth, Va.

CONTENTS

1.

A MIGHTY FORTRESS IS OUR GOD

Martin Luther was depressed. Sickness as well as disappointment laid hold upon him to sap his strength and crush his enthusiasm. Twelve years earlier he had boldly nailed his ninety-five theses to the cathedral door in Wittenberg, Germany. How well he recalled many of the events that had taken place since that memorable event in 1517. He had been excommunicated by the Pope and had defiantly burned the order in public, just as The Holy Father was to order Luther's books burned later on. The debates with Dr. John Eck, the famous Diet at Worms, the translation of the Holy Bible into the common language of the average German, the flood of books that had flowed from his pen, together with his marriage to Katherine von Bora four years before, came clearly to his mind.

But the year 1529 was a sad, heart-breaking time, not only for him personally but for the movement he had set in motion twelve years earlier. In an attempt to snap himself out of his mental and spiritual doldrums, he even took some of his own advice. "Eve got into trouble when she walked in the garden alone. I have my worst temptations when I am by myself," he had written. So he purposely shunned solitude and sought the companionship of like-minded men and women.

"Fasting is the worst expedient," he said. "It is bad enough to be depressed without being hungry." So he found convivial company and ate and drank to his body's content, if not his heart's. Looking over some of his recent volumes, he discovered that he had once written three rules for shaking off dull sloth and despondency: Faith in Christ; Get Mad; Win the love of a good woman. But his favorite medicine was music. "The devil hates music," he said, "because he cannot endure gaiety. Satan can smirk but he cannot laugh; he can sneer but he cannot sing."

11

So he could sing with his family, with his friends, and even when alone.

"When I go to bed, the Devil is always waiting for me," he wrote, so he began ridding himself of his hellish adversary by preaching and singing to him; on some occasions, it worked wonders! "Life is for me a constant struggle for faith," he said. "Sometimes I have to meet the devil head-on and clash openly with him; then again, at other times, I have to meet his challenge indirectly in order to vanquish my enemy."

But in Coburg, in 1529, his forty-fifth year, the depression lingered for days on end, until he thought he would never regain his former confidence and composure again. He tried to understand himself and his moods; undertake some task bigger than himself, hoping that he could save his life by losing it; and undergird his life with the fellowship of the Church. Out of the depths of his agony and despair, he remembered the words Jesus cried from the cross, "My God, my God, why hast thou forsaken me?" He reminded himself that the very cry of despair began with the words, "My God," an affirmation of faith.

This man, who had given back the Bible to his countrymen in their own tongue, had also restored the practice of congregational singing, writing hymns in his own language and composing tunes that he felt his people would love to sing. He made music once more the joy of the entire congregation rather than the sole duty of the choir, and gave it the spontaneity which has always characterized Christian hymnody at its best; he even allowed the women to sing with the others in public, a privilege that had been withheld from them for a thousand years.

In the late summer of 1529, Psalm forty-six was a great comfort to him. He repeated the first verse over and over again, "God is our refuge and strength, a very present help in trouble." With those words burning inside his heart, he hurled his defiance at his enemies, be they pope or peasant, Satan or sin, and penned the account of his struggle in one of the most majestic hymns ever written. As translated by Frederick Hedge in 1853, the hymn contains these superb lines:

A mighty fortress is our God, A bulwark never failing;
Our helper He, amid the flood, Of mortal ills prevailing.

12

For still our ancient foe, Doth seek to work us woe;
His craft and power are great, And armed with cruel hate.
On earth is not his equal.

The four stanzas were reminders that God is the fortress of
the soul; Christ the champion of the soul; and Satan, the enemy
of the soul. But the ultimate victory will be God's whose
"Kingdom is forever."

Author-composer Martin Luther (1483-1546), one of history's outstanding heroes, in no greater way served his own age,
and left to ours no finer legacy, than in writing and composing
"A Mighty Fortress Is Our God."

2.

ABIDE WITH ME

All through his life, Henry Francis Lyte felt that one day he would write something immortal. But when the inspiration finally came, he almost let it slip through his fingers. So weak was he from the ravages of tuberculosis that he nearly postponed polishing up and putting the final touches on his last poem.

"I can do it when I come back," he thought, as he planned a trip to Italy for his health. "I will feel more like working then." But the inner compulsion was not to be denied. So, on September 4, 1847, his fifty-fourth year, he finished the poem he had begun many years earlier, and set forth on his final and fatal journey.

Life had not been easy for Lyte. Poverty plagued his youth, but he managed to complete his training for the ministry, take Holy Orders, and settle down, at twenty-one, in a small parish in Ireland. But even there doubt haunted him and uncertainty dogged his footsteps. He even began questioning his call to the Christian ministry and wondered why he had not followed the medical profession instead. A visit to a dying brother-minister wrought a marvelous transformation in his life, and inspired him to pen his spiritual autobiography in a remarkable hymn which began with these lines:

Jesus, I my cross have taken, All to leave and follow Thee;
Naked, poor, despised, forsaken, Thou from hence my all shalt be.

In that spirit he plunged into his work with increased devotion. In 1823 he was appointed perpetual curate of Lower Brixham, Devon, England, where he labored tirelessly, relinquishing hopes and ambitions to be a "good soldier of Jesus Christ." But even there peace and quiet were denied him. During his frequent absences from the parish in the fruitless search for good health dissensions arose in the Church, members withdrew, and finally even the choir refused to sing.

"I must get away to a dry climate," he often said. "My feeble frame cannot endure much more." But he pushed himself to complete a small booklet, "Spirit of the Psalms," which he published in 1834. This volume included, among other poems, one entitled "Praise, my soul, the king of heaven." Little did he dream that after the passing of more than a century a future Queen of England, Elizabeth II, would choose this as the opening hymn for her wedding to Lieut. Philip Mountbatten, because it had been sung at the wedding of her own parents, King George VI and Queen Elizabeth.

"Twenty-four years is a long time to stay in one parish," the weary pastor said, as he prepared for his trip to the south. "I must put everything in order before I leave because I have no idea how long I will be away," he continued. As he went about the task of packing books, and sorting accumulated papers, sermons and miscellaneous manuscripts, he suddenly discovered in the bottom drawer of his desk, a poem he had written nearly a quarter of a century earlier.

"Strange how appropriate these words are now," he commented, as he read a few of the lines to members of his family. "I remember the night in my first parish, Wrexham, when I was called to the bedside of William Augustus Le Hunte. As he lay dying he kept repeating the words 'Abide with me, abide with me,' possibly from the story of Jesus and the two disciples on the road to Emmaus. After leaving his bedside I wrote this poem and had completely forgotten it until the pages came to light today."

On Sunday, September 4, 1847, he administered the Lord's Supper for the last time. His gardener recalled that after tea at the parsonage, "Berry Head," he walked in the garden in front of the home a while, and then went down on the rocks by the sea where he sat for a long time, working over his manuscript. After the sun had set he returned to his study. His family thought he was resting, but he was putting the final touches on his finest hymn. Later, as they listened reverently, he read them eight stanzas which began:

Abide with me, fast falls the eventide; The darkness deepens,
    Lord with me abide;
When other helpers fail, and comforts flee, Help of the helpless,
    O, abide with me.

He left with his family the very next morning, September 5,
and arrived soon after at Mentone, near Nice, France, at the foot
of the Maritime Alps, in a climate of perpetual sunshine. There
his life slowly ebbed away; he died on November 20, 1847, his
last words being, "Oh, there is nothing terrible in death. Jesus
steps down into the grave before me and I have both peace and
hope." On his gravestone these words are carved:

    Heaven's morning breaks, and earth's vain shadows flee,
    In life, in death, O Lord, abide with me.

He had prayed in an earlier poem, "Grant me, swan-like, my last
breath to spend, In songs that may not die." God granted his
prayer, and years after his death his words are numbered among
the songs that cannot die.

3.

ALAS AND DID MY SAVIOUR BLEED

When the first General Assembly of the Presbyterian Church in the United States of America met in Philadelphia's Second Presbyterian Church in May, 1789, Rev. Adam Rankin was granted permission to speak. "I have ridden on horseback all the way from my home in Kentucky," he said, "to ask this august body to refuse to allow the great and pernicious error of adopting the use of Isaac Watts' hymns in public worship in preference to Rouse's versifications of the Psalms of David."

The Assembly heard him patiently, and, with Calvinistic wisdom, requested him to "exercise Christian charity toward those who differ from him in their views." They further suggested that he be "guarded against disturbing the peace of the Church on this matter."

So while the hymns of Watts (who died in 1748) are now considered standard, superb and sublime, they were not so regarded by some leaders of his own generation and century. Nevertheless, this remarkable bachelor should be honored by posterity if only because he wrote one of the loveliest hymns for little children ever penned. Not having children of his own, he had the time to write a stanza with which other parents sing their "little angels" to sleep:

Hush, my dear, lie still and slumber, Holy angels guard thy bed;
Heavenly blessings without number, Gently falling on thy head.

His life was far from dull and early he became adjusted to upsets and disappointments. Twice during his infancy and early boyhood, his father was imprisoned for refusing to attend the Established Church, choosing rather to worship with a fellowship of non-conformists led by Rev. Nathaniel Robinson. On both occasions his mother took the lad with her when she sat outside

17

the prison walls to converse or sing with her husband who took part from the other side of the bars.

Years later he corresponded with Miss Elizabeth Singer, who had written him of her admiration for his poetry, and felt that he had met his soul-mate at last. But when they met, she saw him as a little man "only five feet tall with a sallow face, hooked nose, prominent cheek bones, small eyes and deathlike color," and refused his proposal of marriage. She said, "I admired the jewel but not the casket." Possibly he wrote these lines shortly thereafter:

How vain are all things here below, How false and yet so fair.

While Fanny Crosby did not write her first hymn until she was forty-four, Watts wrote his last famous hymn at the same age, spending the rest of his years writing on theological and controversial matters. As a preacher he was outstanding in a day that boasted many leading orators. A contemporary wrote, "Though his stature was low and his bodily presence weak, yet his preaching was weighty and powerful." He preached his first sermon when twenty-four, and became assistant and then minister of the Independent Church in Mark Lane, London, which post he filled for ten years. Ill-health forced him to resign, and it was then that he retired to the home of Lord Mayor of London, Sir Thomas, and Lady Abney, where he spent the rest of his days.

His first book of hymns was published in 1705, his thirty-first year, followed two years later by "Hymns and Spiritual Songs." It was in this volume that a new hymn, "Godly Sorrow Arising from the Sufferings of Christ" appeared for the first time. The opening stanza read:

Alas! and did my Saviour bleed, And did my Sovereign die?
Would He devote that sacred head, For such a worm as I?

While this generation substitutes "sinners such as I" for the original, confident that we are not worms, it is well to remember that a worm is the only thing in God's world that can change into a butterfly. And Watts well knew that the transformation wrought in the human heart by the grace of God whereby the "old man" dies and the "new man in Christ Jesus" is born, finds its parallel in the process of nature whereby a worm dies that a butterfly may be born!

Later, in "Psalms of David," published in 1719, he included a poem on the shortest chapter in the Bible, Psalm 117, which began, "From all that dwell below the skies." This same volume contained his metrical version of Psalm 90, "O God our help in ages past" and Psalm 98, "Joy to the world, the Lord is come."

In an age that frowned upon original stanzas, and which believed that God stopped singing when David died, Watts dared to prove that God still sang as He had in every past age and would continue to in ages yet unborn, and single-handedly rescued hymnody from the prison-house of the Old Testament. By himself he set in motion a movement that will live as long as Christians are inspired to raise their hearts and lift their voices in praise to God.

4.

AMAZING GRACE

Most Christians who sing "Amazing grace, how sweet the sound, That saved a wretch like me," don't feel like wretches at all. But the author of the hymn, John Newton, did. And if ever there was a wretch who was marvelously saved by the grace of God, it was the man who penned those autobiographical lines.

London-born John Newton, only child of a respectable sea-captain father, was early dedicated to the Christian ministry by his devout, consumptive mother. His religious training began almost at once, and, by the time he was four, he could recite passages from the Westminster Catechism and the children's hymns of Isaac Watts. At eleven he was sailing the Mediterranean with his father, but at seventeen he laid aside every religious principle and abandoned himself to the service of the devil. Only his love for Mary Catlett, with whom he fell in love in 1742 but did not marry until 1750, kept a few sparks of decency aglow within his heart.

He deserted his ship, was caught and brought back like a common felon. So severe was his punishment that he plotted suicide, his great love for Mary being the restraining influence that preserved his life. After his imprisonment, he embarked on a career of such wickedness that his friends despaired of his sanity.

Living for a time among the cruel slavers of Sierra Leone, he was mistreated by his Portuguese master's black wife. Of these days, he said, "Had you seen me go so pensive and solitary in the dead of night to wash my one shirt upon the rocks and afterward to put it on wet that it might dry on my back while I slept; had you seen me so poor a figure than when a ship's boat came to the island, shame often constrained me to hide myself in the woods from the sight of strangers; had you known that my conduct, principles and heart were still darker than my outward condition—how little would you have imagined that such a one was reserved to be so peculiar an instance of the providential care and exuberant goodness of God."

Later he added, "The only good desire I had left was to get back to England to marry Mary."

After further humiliation and suffering, he boarded a vessel for England, spending several quiet days at sea reading "Imitation of Christ." When a violent storm arose, he regarded himself as the Jonah who was the cause and blamed his wicked life for the raging winds and mountainous seas that threatened to engulf the vessel. Suddenly a storm as violent as nature's broke over his soul. With awakened conscience he regarded that day, March 10, 1748, as his "spiritual birthday."

"I cried to the Lord with a cry like that of the ravens which yet the Lord does not disdain to hear," he said. "And I remembered Jesus whom I had so often derided."

But the change that took place was only the reformation of an unconverted man. During the next six years he made several voyages as captain of his own ship, even carrying cargoes of slaves on some occasions. Not until he reached Liverpool in August, 1754, did he consider himself a regenerated Christian. But even then he did not feel the call to the ministry to which his godly mother had so early set him apart. Gradually he came to consecrate everything to Christ, in the hope that he might be deemed worthy of being called into His service. After two miraculous escapes from death, and several years of hard study and training, he was appointed a minister of the Church of England on December 16, 1758. Six years later he went to Olney, where he was ordained a deacon and a priest. His fellowship with William Cowper resulted in the publication of their "Olney Hymns." Number forty-one, of Book I, contained Newton's life-story in this form:

Amazing grace, how sweet the sound, That saved a wretch like me;
I once was lost but now am found, Was blind but now I see.
'Twas grace that taught my heart to fear, And grace my fears relieved;

How precious did that grace appear, The hour I first believed.
Through many dangers, toils and snares, I have already come;
'Tis grace hath brought me safe thus far, And grace will lead
me home.

He made his last move in 1779, going to serve two churches in London. There he labored faithfully until his death, December 21, 1807, at the age of eighty-two. His epitaph, which he wrote himself, reads as follows:

"JOHN NEWTON, Clerk, once an infidel and libertine, was, by the rich mercy of our Lord and Saviour, JESUS CHRIST, preserved, restored, pardoned and appointed to preach the faith he had long labored to destroy, near sixteen years at Olney in Bucks, and twenty-eight years in this Church."

Later he added, "And I earnestly desire that no other monument and no inscription but to this purport, may be attempted for me."

5.

AMERICA

Samuel Francis Smith was too young and inexperienced to write a hymn. How could he, at twenty-four, be expected to write anything that would be accepted by his countrymen and Church, much less a poem that would be more popular a hundred years after his death than during his life? Yet in 1832, he did it not only once, but three times.

This Boston-born youth, a graduate of Harvard in 1829, entered Andover Theological Seminary to prepare himself for the Baptist ministry. He had already begun to distinguish himself as a master of German, and was trying his hand successfully at translating poems from that language into his own. One afternoon in February, 1832, his twenty-fourth year, he had a visitor in his room at Andover, forty-year-old Lowell Mason, musician, composer, teacher and hymnologist. The young student was curious to know the reason for the visit and Dr. Mason hastened to explain. "As you doubtless know," he began, "I have been working on a plan to introduce the study of music in the public schools of Massachusetts." The young man nodded and Dr. Mason continued. "After several years of planning, I realized that many people were somewhat sceptical about including the study of music in the high school curricula. So I altered my tactics and approached the problem from another angle."

"How was that, Dr. Mason?"

"A group of us finally succeeded in securing funds from the Legislature to enable us to send a commission to study public school music in England and on the continent of Europe. William C. Woodbridge was chosen to head this commission."

"The well-known geographer?"

"Yes. Under his direction studies were made in several countries, principally Germany. In his travels, Mr. Woodbridge collected a tremendous amount of material, papers, manuscripts, booklets, pamphlets, songs, tunes and nearly everything imaginable."

"Where do I fit into the picture?" young Smith asked.

"Well, the men returned home a few weeks ago. I've been looking through some of their papers, but, since I am not a student of German, much of what they brought is just so much Greek to me. I carried some of the documents with me today, hoping you would agree to look through them at your leisure and advise us what to keep and what to discard."

"That's quite a responsibility, Doctor; but I'll do what I can."

"We have faith not only in your ability, Mr. Smith, but also in your good judgement."

"I'll be careful," young Smith promised, and Dr. Mason went his way.

A few days later Smith began browsing through the papers and found little of unusual merit until he came across a patriotic poem in German which began:

God bless our native land; Firm may she ever stand, In storm and night.

He noticed that the poem was written in the rather unusual 6.6.4.6.6.6.4. meter. (The numerals indicate the number of syllables in each line of the poem. This one has seven lines with six and four syllables in that order.) He was not surprised to find a melody shortly thereafter to which the song could be sung. The music as well as the peculiar meter of the poem impressed him, and he suddenly decided to try his hand at a patriotic poem in his own tongue to be sung to the same tune. Hurriedly he jotted down four stanzas, the first of which read:

My country, 'tis of thee, Sweet land of liberty; Of thee I sing.
Land where my father died; Land of the pilgrim's pride;
From every mountain-side, Let freedom ring.

Five months later, Dr. Mason had his Junior Choir introduce the new patriotic hymn at a special Fourth of July service in Park Street Church, Boston, where he was organist and choir director. It was received with acclaim and enthusiasm and its immediate popularity made Samuel F. Smith famous almost overnight. The fact that the tune was the one to which the British sang their national anthem, "God Save the King," seemed but a closer tie between the mother country and her daughter.

The author served as pastor of several Baptist churches in Maine and Massachusetts, following which he devoted himself exclusively to the secretarial and editorial work of the American Baptist Missionary Union, serving in that capacity from 1854 until his death in 1895. Although he wrote over a hundred hymns, including the other two he penned that same year, 1832 (the Sunday evening hymn "Softly Fades the Twilight Ray" and the missionary hymn "The Morning Light is Breaking"), none attained the wide use and popularity of "America." "For its easy grace, its directness and simplicity, its zealous patriotism, its fervent piety and its insistent note of liberty, it has become the favorite national hymn."

6.

AMERICA THE BEAUTIFUL

Every school child knows that "Columbus sailed the ocean blue in fourteen-hundred and ninety-two." But very few of them know that the celebration of the four-hundredth anniversary of his discovery inspired a school teacher to write one of our noblest patriotic hymns.

In connection with this nation-wide observance, the city of Chicago sponsored the Columbian Exposition, a World's Fair of yesterday, which ran continuously for several years. On the site of the Exposition magnificent buildings were erected. Every structure designed by Daniel Burnham was a masterpiece of planning, construction and beauty. Thousands of people came from all over the world to marvel at the splendor and stand enraptured before the grandeur of such a spectacle.

In the early summer of 1893, while the Exposition was still in full swing, a group of teachers and professors from Wellesley, a famous girls' college, stopped off in Chicago enroute to Colorado. Among them was thirty-four-year-old Katharine Lee Bates, holder of a Master's Degree from Oxford, and a professor of English. The young women were profoundly impressed by all they saw in and about "The Windy City"; but they soon left Lake Michigan behind them as they continued their journey westward. Once in Colorado, they made the trip up the famous peak which was named for the American general who discovered it about 1806, Zebulon Montgomery Pike. From the summit, which towers more than fourteen-thousand feet above sea level, Miss Bates "gazed in wordless rapture over the expanse of mountain ranges and the sealike sweep of the plains" that stretched before her for hundreds of miles until they seemed to melt into the misty blue of heaven.

Later that evening, the teachers were talking over the events

26

of the day in the home in which they were staying in Colorado Springs. The discussion naturally included a comparison of the Exposition, a man-made spectacle, with the Rocky Mountains and the view from Pike's Peak, fashioned by the hand of God. Miss Bates suggested that "unless we crown our good with brotherhood, of what lasting benefit are our spacious skies, our amber waves of grain, our mountain majesties or our fruited plains." She added, "We must match the greatness of our America with the goodness of personal godly living." Soon the teachers were comparing the land of their day with the America of the Pilgrims and the Jamestown settlers of 1607. They spoke of the two stones that played important parts in the nation's history; the Ten Commandments and Plymouth Rock, and agreed that if their fellow-citizens could couple the daring of the Pilgrims with the moral teachings of Moses, together with the ability of them both to venture into uncharted seas, they would really have something in this country that no one could ever take from them.

They mentioned the heroes and heroines of the past, from Molly Pitcher to Barbara Fritchie, and felt that it is more difficult to be a living hero in one's own day than to revere a dead hero from a former day. When one teacher showed the group a small piece of alabaster she had purchased in a souvenir shop, the others talked about "the alabaster city" where all would be joy and peace, and where people would live together with their eyes undimmed by human tears. Later that night, with the events of the trip vividly in her mind, Miss Bates sat down and expressed her dream of a Christian nation in these words:

O beautiful for spacies skies, For amber waves of grain;
For purple mountain majesties, Above the fruited plain.
America! America! God shed His grace on thee;
And crown thy good with brotherhood, From sea to shining sea.

Before she laid her pen down she had written four stanzas, each closing with a prayer for her beloved America. The stanzas were not printed until two years after they were written. In the July 4, 1895 issue of "The Congregationalist" they appeared for the first time outside her own private notebook. Quickly they were accepted, quoted, and widely acclaimed as an expression of Christian patriotism at its highest and best. Of the many musical settings, one has endured—the hymn tune "Materna" which Samuel A. Ward composed for the hymn "O Mother Dear Jerusalem." Today this tune and her stanzas are wedded in the hearts of the American people.

The author was honored with degrees from many colleges and universities. During her forty-five years as a professor and before her death in 1929, she wrote seventeen books. But she is loved and honored today as the author of one of the nation's finest patriotic hymns. If the celebration of the four-hundredth anniversary of the discovery of America did no more than inspire Rev. Francis Bellamy to write the original "Pledge of Allegiance to the Flag" and Katharine Lee Bates to write "America the Beautiful" it was eminently worthwhile. Because the Pledge and the Poem will live as long as America lives.

7.

ANOTHER YEAR IS DAWNING

Since most verses on New Year greeting cards are so much sentimental "slush," if such a versifier ever produced a poem that would last from a year's beginning until its end, it would be little short of miraculous. But if such a poem actually became a well-known and widely-used hymn, that would be news of a sensational nature. And if the same poet did it for two consecutive years, that would almost defy description.

But that is precisely what England's most famous woman hymn-writer, Frances Ridley Havergal, did. For ushering in the year 1873, she penned a stirring bit of poetry which contained these lines:

> Standing at the portal, Of the opening year,
> Words of comfort meet us, Hushing every fear;
> Spoken through the silence, By our Father's voice,
> Tender, strong and faithful, Making us rejoice.
> Onward then, and fear not, Children of the day;
> For His word shall never, Never pass away.

For the same season the very next year, 1874, when she was thirty-six years of age, she dashed off another original poem, had it printed on a specially designed greeting card and sent it to her friends under this caption, "A Happy New Year! Ever such may it be!" These stanzas now comprise one of our noblest hymns for welcoming in the year; its equal would be hard to find. Beginning with this couplet:

> Another year is dawning, Dear Master, let it be,
> In working or in waiting, Another year for Thee;—it

closes with these two lines:

> Another year is dawning, Dear Master, let it be
> On earth or else in heaven, Another year for Thee.

Although she did not have to write verses for a living, she did it for the sheer joy of expressing her Christian faith. Blessed with a beautiful voice, and skilled as a pianist, this "ten-talent woman" used all of her gifts in the glad service of "The King of Kings." Author of more than seven volumes, and at home in at least six languages, she early committed the entire New Testament and Book of Psalms to memory. While she suffered from ill-health for many years, and was coddled by her family on that account, her poems and hymns abound in verbs denoting action and activity. Her thrilling hymn-tune "Hermas" is found in many Hymnals; to it we sing either her hymn "Golden Harps Are Sounding" or the thrilling Easter hymn, "Welcome, Happy Morning." As for her hymns, she gave God all the credit for their composition.

"I believe my King suggests a thought," she wrote, "and whispers me a musical line or two, and then I look up and thank Him delightedly and go on with it. That is how my hymns come."

Although she died in 1879, at forty-two, just five years after writing her famous prayer-poem for the New Year, she left a rich legacy of sacred verse, including such gems as "I Gave My Life for Thee" (her first successful hymn), "Lord, Speak to Me that I May Speak," "Who Is on the Lord's Side?," and the one that is most descriptive of her own experience, "Take My Life and Let It Be, Consecrated, Lord, to Thee."

8

BLESSED ASSURANCE, JESUS IS MINE

Holders of life-insurance policies in the Metropolitan Life Insurance Company may not know the name of the distinguished American who founded the firm, but millions of Church-goers are familiar with some of the music composed by his equally distinguished wife. Married to Joesph Fairchild Knapp, who was prominent enough to be offered the nomination for Mayor of New York City, and mother of Joseph Palmer Knapp, who at the time of his death in 1951 at the age of eighty-six was head of the Crowell-Collier Publishing Company, one of the nation's leading publishers of magazines and periodicals, Phoebe Palmer Knapp is beloved by Christians the world over.

This daughter of evangelist Dr. Walter Palmer and his wife, Phoebe, was born in New York City in 1839 and early displayed unusual musical talent. Her marriage to Knapp was described as "an ideal one in every way." Both were members of the St. John's Methodist Church, being active, consistent and liberal Christians. It was in 1873 that this gifted woman visited Fanny Crosby, the blind hymn-writer who was to become one of the most prolific poets of all time. The author records this memorable visit in these words, "My dear friend, Mrs. Joseph F. Knapp, so well-known as a writer and singer of most excellent music, and as an aid and inspiration to all who knew her, had composed the tune, and it seemed to me one of the sweetest I had heard for a long time. She asked me to write a hymn for it, and I felt while bringing the words and tones together that the air and the hymn were intended for each other."

That she was right in her assumption is evidenced by the universal regard in which her stanzas are held. The lines, written to fit the music, began:

31

Blessed assurance, Jesus is mine; O what a foretaste of glory divine.
Heir of salvation, purchase of God; Born of His Spirit, washed in His blood.

CHORUS:

This is my story, this is my song; Praising my Saviour all the day long;
This is my story, this is my song; Praising my Saviour all the day long.

At the death of her husband in 1891, Mrs. Knapp was left an annual income of some $50,000.00, much of which was dispensed in charitable and philanthropic work. Later these two remarkable women produced the solo which is associated with Easter Sunday, "Open the Gates of the Temple," Fanny Crosby writing the words and her friend composing the music.

Her son, thrice-wed sportsman, possessed his mother's generous spirit, and gave widely to many worthy causes, generally through the Knapp Foundation, Incorporated, of New York and North Carolina. Although born in Brooklyn, in a home in which Union Generals Grant and Sheridan had been entertained as guests, he presented to Currituck County, North Carolina, a Confederate monument, specifying, however, that there was to be no statue of a soldier.

Mrs. Knapp, "sweet singer, accomplished organist and earnest Christian worker," died at Poland Springs, Maine, July 10, 1908. History may record that the memory and influence of the wife of the founder of a great life insurance company, and the mother of one of the country's leading publishers, outlived that of her famous husband and son; and the name "Knapp" may be remembered because of "Blessed Assurance" and "Open the Gates of the Temple."

9.

BLEST BE THE TIE THAT BINDS

After seven years as minister of the Baptist Church in Wainsgate, England, Rev. John Fawcett wrote these words in his diary, in the summer of 1772, "During these years our family has increased faster than our income." When a messenger arrived a few weeks later with a "call" from the famous Carter's Lane Baptist Church in London, it seemed like an answer to prayer.

"Think of it," the bewildered clergyman said to his family, "they want us up in London, to take the place of the late Dr. Gill at that great Church. It's almost unbelievable!"

And it was. But the good minister sent a letter of acceptance as soon as he could draft a favorable reply, and dispatched the messenger back to the capital city in a hurry. The following Sunday he told his parishioners about the "call" and the answer in which his entire family had concurred. His people were loath to give him up, though, and hoped against hope for a miracle to prevent his departure.

The next few days were unusually busy ones; everyone worked hard packing books and dishes, discarding odds and ends, and crating furniture for the overland journey to the largest city in the world. Members of the Church joined in, albeit with little enthusiasm. A deep feeling of loyalty and mutual devotion between pastor and people had developed during the recent years, and most of his faithful flock were frightened at the prospect of tearing asunder such precious ties. But they willingly did what they could to make his leaving easier. On the appointed day the wagons arrived early. Some people stood about the yard as if to delay the actual loading, but others began moving the boxes and bundles from the house as members of the family engaged in their final farewells.

Then only one large box in the middle of the dining room remained. The pastor entered the room and saw his wife standing nearby, deep in thought.

"What's the matter?" he asked.

She hesitated a moment. "John," she answered slowly, "do you think we are doing the right thing in leaving Wainsgate for London?"

"Why do you ask?"

She stepped forward and took his hand. "John, dear, will we ever find a congregation to love us and help with us in the Lord's work like this group here?"

He asked, "Do you mean to say that you think we've been too hasty in all this?"

"Yes," she said. "I think we should stay right here and serve these people and give up all thought of going to London."

After an awkward silence he added, "And I think so, too. I was so overjoyed when the 'call' came that I never really prayed about it like a minister should. I just thought of a better home for the family, the larger salary and the advantages of living in a big city."

"We are happy wherever you are happy, dear," she replied.

They walked out on the porch and explained their change of mind. In a short while the wagons were unloaded and everything was safely and securely back in place. The pastor sent another letter to the London congregation telling them of the events of the day and asking them to concur in his new decision to remain at Wainsgate.

And for his own people, with the happenings of the week in mind, he penned the most beautiful hymn of Christian brotherhood ever written. It begins with these lines:

> Blest be the tie that binds, Our hearts in Christian love;
> The fellowship of kindred minds, Is like to that above.

And Rev. John Fawcett stayed at Wainsgate for the next forty-five years, until his death, July 25, 1817.

10.

BREAK THOU THE BREAD OF LIFE

If Mary A. Lathbury had not done such an excellent job in writing a vesper hymn for use at the Chautauqua, New York, religious conferences, she would not have been asked to write what has become one of the best hymns about the Bible in all hymnody. She had served in an editorial capacity for Rev. John H. Vincent when he was Secretary of the Methodist Sunday School Union, and through him she became associated with the Chautauqua movement. Thus it was that she spent the summer of her thirty-fifth year at the summer assembly ground on beautiful Lake Chautauqua in the finger lakes region of western New York state.

William F. Sherwin, director of music, and his assistant, George Stebbins, little dreamed that that particular summer of 1877 would be one of the most fruitful in their lives. At Bishop Vincent's request, Miss Lathbury wrote the well-known evening hymn "Day Is Dying in the West" for which Mr. Sherwin immediately composed his equally famous tune "Chautauqua—Evening Praise," to which her stanzas are universally sung. A more perfect wedding of words and music would be hard to find. Becoming instantly popular, this hymn has found its way into most of the hymnals of English-speaking Christendom.

Because the Chautauqua Literary and Scientific Circle had sponsored study classes which were becoming increasingly popular, Bishop Vincent was encouraged to suggest to the "lyrist of Chautauqua" that she and Mr. Sherwin collaborate on another new hymn for this organization.

"They emphasize the study of the Bible as well as related fields, such as archaeology, ancient history, science, literature and philosophy," he explained. "The president of the group asked me to make this request of the two of you," he added, "so the members can use the new hymn in connection with their morning class sessions."

When Mr. Sherwin agreed to compose the music, Miss Lathbury could not turn the director down.

There was a dearth of good hymns about the Bible, the poet soon learned. Bishop How had written "O Word of God Incarnate" ten years earlier, in 1867, but Rev. Washington Gladden was not to pen his hymn, "Behold a Sower from Afar" until 1904. It was her good fortune to fasten upon a theme that had not yet been developed in hymns about the Bible, that of "Christ, the bread of life, breaking for His children the living bread in His Book, just as He broke the physical bread for the hungry by the shores of the Galilean lake centuries ago." With that idea in mind, the talented "poet laureate" wrote several stanzas, the first of which contained these lines:

> Break thou the bread of life, Dear Lord to me,
> As thou did'st break the loaves Beside the sea;
> Beyond the sacred page I seek thee, Lord;
> My spirit pants for thee, O living Word.

Mr. Sherwin rose to the occasion with a tune he named significantly "Bread of Life."

While the poet wrote widely on a variety of subjects and the musician composed many other tunes for hymns and songs, they are remembered today for the unusual collaboration of that summer of 1877 which produced the two Chautauqua hymns, "Day Is Dying in the West" and "Break Thou the Bread of Life." Although the latter has often been misused as a Communion hymn, it is found in the section on "The Holy Scriptures" in most Hymnals today, and continues to be the favorite hymn about the Bible in the hearts of millions who cherish and study the Word of God. And by most of them it will be sung reverently, prayerfully and enthusiastically on the second Sunday in December which has been designated "Universal Bible Sunday."

11.

COME THOU FOUNT OF EVERY BLESSING

"Give her some more liquor, boys," the young man said. The poor gipsy woman was already so drunk she could hardly stand on her feet. But the wild and reckless young men were determined to get her even more drunk.

"Pour it into her, and we'll get her to tell our fortunes," seventeen-year-old Robert Robinson shouted. The others plied her with more intoxicants until she agreed to predict their futures for nothing.

"She doesn't know what she's saying; she's drunk," one rowdy exclaimed, after she had prophesied that evil fortune awaited him. "You ought to know," Robinson replied. "You gave it to her."

Turning to the self-appointed leader, the bleary-eyed gipsy pointed a quivering finger and said, "And you, young man, you will live to see your children and your grandchildren." Robinson suddenly paled and said, "You're right. She's too drunk to know what she's saying. Leave her alone. Let's go."

But her words haunted him the rest of the day. "If I'm going to live to see my children and grandchildren," he thought, "I'll have to change my way of living. I can't keep on like I'm going now." So, that very night, half in fun and half seriously, he took his gang to an open air revival service nearby where the famous evangelist, George Whitfield, was preaching. "We'll go down and laugh at the poor deluded Methodists," he explained.

But the Spirit of God was already at work in the troubled heart and confused mind of the wayward youth. That night Whitfield preached from Matthew 3:7, "O generation of vipers, who hath warned you to flee from the wrath to come?" The message sobered and frightened him at the same time. He felt that the preacher was speaking to him and only to him. On

Tuesday, December 10, 1755, two years and seven months after hearing that sermon, twenty-year-old Robert Robinson made his peace with God, and "found full and free forgiveness through the precious blood of Jesus Christ." He later wrote the preacher who had first convicted him of his sinfulness, "I confess it was to spy the nakedness of the land I came—to pity the folly of the preacher, the infatuation of the hearers, and to abhor the doctrine. I went pitying the poor deluded Methodists but came away envying their happiness."

Joining the Methodists, and feeling the call to preach, self-taught Robinson was appointed by John Wesley to the Calvinist Methodist Chapel, Norfolk, England. There, for the celebration of Pentecost (Whitsunday), in 1858, three years after his marvelous conversion, he penned his spiritual autobiography in these lines:

Come, thou fount of every blessing, Tune my heart to sing thy
    grace;
Streams of mercy, never ceasing, Call for songs of loudest praise.
Teach me some melodious sonnet, Sung by flaming tongues
    above;
Praise the mount—I'm fixed upon it, Mount of thy redeeming
    love!

Recalling that Samuel, after a battle in which the Philistine enemy had been routed, took a stone and "set it between Mizpeh and Shen, and called the name of it Ebenezer, saying, Hitherto hath the Lord helped us" (I Samuel 7:12), he felt that he should raise a spiritual Ebenezer in his own heart to commemorate the victory of God over Satan three years earlier. Realizing that it was only by God's help that he had been saved and dedicated to the ministry, he wanted that "symbolic stone" to remind him that "hither by thy help I'm come." So he wrote a stanza containing these lines:

Here I'll raise my Ebenezer, Hither by thy help I'm come,
  And I hope by thy good pleasure Safely to arrive at home.

This hymn, published a year later in a volume entitled, "A Collection of Hymns Used by the Church of Christ in Angel Alley, Bishopsgate," became the most popular one Robinson ever wrote. In December of that same year, he wrote a Christmas hymn at the personal request of a lad in his congregation. With slight adaptations to make it appropriate for adults to sing, we know it as "Mighty God, while angels bless thee, May a mortal lisp thy name?"

At various times a Methodist, an "open communion" Baptist, an Independent and a Unitarian, he is spoken of as a rare preacher who could say "what he pleased, when he pleased and how he pleased." The author of numerous books, he had to buy a farm and manage it on the side in order to provide for the needs of his growing family. He died as he wished to die, on June 9, 1790, at the age of fifty-five, "soft, suddenly and alone."

12.

FATHER WHATE'ER OF EARTHLY BLISS

If any woman had just cause to be bitter and rebellious toward God it was Anne Steele (1716-1788). Born at Broughton, Hampshire, England, the daughter of a wealthy timber-merchant and part-time Baptist preacher, William Steele, she lost her mother when she was only three years old. This very delicate girl, who was threatened with tuberculosis all her life, united with the Church at fourteen. Early she began writing hymns and poems, and often entertained her friends by reading or reciting her own compositions.

When she was nineteen she suffered another shock when a serious injury to her hip left her practically an invalid. Much of her time was spent in her own room, and for days at a time she was confined to her bed, totally helpless. But she met a young man, Robert Elscourt, and they fell in love. When she was twenty-one, they set the day for their wedding, but he was tragically drowned the evening before the scheduled marriage was to take place. But even his untimely death and the delicate condition of her own health did not embitter her. Like Joseph Scriven (author of "What a friend we have in Jesus") whose fiancee also was drowned the evening before their wedding day, her sorrow only served to deepen her faith in God and strengthen her trust in Him.

She poured out her grief in her hymns and poems and the sweetness they embody is in direct contrast to the bitterness of her heart-break. Despite the misery that life seemed to be heaping upon her and the burdens beyond her strength that she was being compelled to bear, she never forgot that God was still her Father. Like the Master, who from the agony of the Cross began the first and last of His Seven Words with the cry "Father," Anne Steele, out of the depths of personal suffering that could neither be denied nor explained, wrote her spiritual autobiography in these majestic lines, entitled, "Desiring Resignation and Thankfulness":

Father, whate'er of earthly bliss Thy sov'reign will denies,
Accepted at Thy throne of grace, Let this petition rise:
Give me a calm, a thankful heart, From every murmur free;
The blessings of Thy grace impart, And let me live to Thee.

This confident and cheerful disposition remained with her the rest of her life. And this faith is seen in the first lines of two other hymns from her pen, which attest to her experience of the reality of God's presence, "Father of Mercies, in Thy Word," and "Dear Father, to Thy Mercy Seat."

Like Isaac Watts, the great hymn writer who lived only fifteen miles from her home, she never married. Since many of her hymns were the result of her own profound and moving experiences, she hesitated to share them with the public. But her family and friends prevailed upon her and it was after she was forty years old that she submitted some of them for publication. Even then she did not send them in under her own name, but the penname "Theodosia." The day she mailed off her first collection of poems, her father wrote in his diary, "This day Nanny sent part of her composition to London to be printed. I entreat a gracious God, who enabled and stirred her up such a work, to direct it, and bless it for the good of many. I pray God to make it useful and to keep her humble."

In 1760 two little volumes appeared, entitled "Poems on Subjects Chiefly Devotional by Theodosia." When Addison and Steele printed some of her poems in their pioneer newspaper "The Spectator" and signed them "Steele," many readers assumed they were the writings of Sir Richard Steele, the coeditor. But he disclaimed the honor and soon the readers learned the identity of the retiring English lady and read her lyrics with more sincere interest than before.

Prior to her death, she wrote 144 hymns, 34 metrical versions of the Psalms and 30 miscellaneous poems, all of which were published in one volume as late as 1863. Considering the number of her hymns and the frequency with which they were sung, she stands out as the leading Baptist hymn-writer of the eighteenth century.

The publication of her slender volumes encouraged other women of like talent to write, and the success of her books opened up to womankind a field of expression previously denied them. In the intervening years, Frances Havergal and Charlotte Elliott have enriched Christian hymnody and put all Christendom in their debt. But they would possibly have hesitated to offer their writings for publication had it not been for the pioneering spirit of Anne Steele.

She died in the same house in which she was born in November 1778. On her tombstone in Broughton Churchyard is this inscription:

> Silent the lyre, and dumb the tuneful tongue
> That sung on earth her great Redeemer's praise;
> But now in heaven she joins the angels' songs
> In more harmonious, more exalted lays.

13.

FROM GREENLAND'S ICY MOUNTAINS

A missionary has never written a great missionary hymn. But in 1819 a young Anglican clergyman wrote a missionary hymn at the request of his father-in-law, little dreaming that four years later he himself would be destined to go to a foreign country to preach and there to die.

On Friday afternoon before Whitsunday (Pentecost), 1819, thirty-six-year-old Reginald Heber was sitting in the study of his father-in-law, Dean Shipley, vicar of Wrexham, an ancient town in North Wales, discussing the sermon the older man planned to preach on Sunday.

The Dean said to his son-in-law, "Reginald, next Sunday we are to receive an offering for the 'Society for the Propagation of the Gospel in Foreign Countries.' "

"What will you preach about?" the younger man asked.

Dean Shipley replied, "The Great Commission, of course. 'Go ye into all the world and preach the gospel to every creature.' I have my sermon about ready but I need an interesting story or poem with which to conclude."

He looked up at his guest, smiled, and said, "Reginald, what's the good of having a brilliant poet for a son-in-law if he can't help his father-in-law out in such a time as this?"

"What do you mean?"

"Just this. Write a missionary poem that I can read as I close my sermon Sunday. After all, it isn't as if you never had written poetry before."

The older man was right. Reginald early had displayed unusual literary gifts. In 1800, as a youth of 17, he had won a coveted prize at Oxford University with a long and remarkable poem on Palestine; it had received such applause as never had been heard before in that sedate gathering.

"But, Dean Shipley—" the young man protested.

"Enough of that," the Dean interrupted; "and while you are at it, make it a hymn instead of a poem, one we can sing as well as read."

To placate the older man, Reginald Heber took a piece of paper and a pen, sat down at a small table nearby and, after a few moments of deep thought, began to write. Fifteen minutes passed before either man spoke, the silence being broken only by the scratching of Heber's pen on the paper.

"I have three stanzas, Dean Shipley," Heber said. "Would you like to hear them?"

"By all means. Read them," the older man commanded. Heber read the first stanza of his first hymn:

From Greenland's icy mountains, From India's coral strand;
Where Afric's sunny fountains, Roll down their golden sand;
From many an ancient river, From many a palmy plain,
They call us to deliver Their land from error's chain.

When he finished the third stanza, Dean Shipley nodded his head in approval. "Magnificent; thrilling; challenging! The entire service will be worthwhile if I do nothing but read those three stanzas."

But the poet shook his head. "It is incomplete. A note of victory is lacking. Let me try my hand at a fourth and final stanza," he explained.

"Leave it alone," the other man protested. "Another stanza would spoil everything."

But the author was not to be denied. "Go on with your studying," he said, "while I work on the closing stanza."

"Well, if you insist, have your way," the Dean commented. "If the final stanza compares with the others, I will be agreeably surprised."

After another short period of silence, meditation and writing, Heber said enthusiastically, "I have it now. Listen. See how this stanza brings the poem to a grand climax."

"All right," the Dean replied. "But I have my doubts."
Heber read aloud:

Waft, waft ye winds His story, And you, ye waters, roll;
Till, like a sea of glory, It spreads from pole to pole:

44

Till, o'er our ransomed nature, The Lamb for sinners slain,
Redeemer, King, Creator, In bliss returns to reign.

The greatest missionary hymn of the 19th century was read for the first time in Wrexham Church, North Wales, on Whitsunday, 1819. In 1823, four years later, a woman in England found a copy of the stanzas in a religious journal and sent it to a friend in Savannah, Georgia. This lady sent the poem to a thirty-one-year-old musical bank clerk who worked a few doors from her home.

In half an hour he returned the poem with an original tune he had composed as spontaneously as Heber had written the stanzas. The composer was Lowell Mason, who became the Father of American Hymnology.

Also in 1823, Heber accepted the appointment as Bishop of Calcutta, his parish including not only all of India, but the island of Ceylon and the whole of Australia. He died there very suddenly in April, 1826. Many of his greatest hymns were published after his death by his wife in a volume entitled "Hymns Written and Adapted to the Weekly Service of the Year."

14.

GOD BE WITH YOU TILL WE MEET AGAIN

The white minister who was to become president of a great Negro university picked up a dictionary in his study at the First Congregational Church, Washington, D.C. He thumbed through the pages until he found what he wanted, and then made some notes on a pad at his side: "Farewell—fare thee well. Wherever you go, whatever you do, however circumstances affect you, may you fare well." Another volume furnished an interpretation of the slang expression, "So Long," and hinted that it was possibly an English corruption of the Mohammedan greeting, "Salaam Alaikum" which means "Peace be with you." Noting that the French farewell, "Adieu" or "Au Revoir," means "Till we meet again," he then looked up the word "Goodbye." He jotted down these notes: "Goodbye—God be with you. Can God go with everyone? Suppose they don't want Him to go with them? Is this not a parting word for Christians only?"

With that he looked up the various "Farewells" in the New Testament and found these references: Acts 15:29, "Fare ye well"; Acts 23:30, "Farewell." From the original Greek, he discovered that these words have a wide variety of meaning, including "God make you strong; be strong; be well; be firm; enjoy good health; rejoice; be joyful and be full of joy."

Since his Sunday evening congregations were growing, the resourceful pastor, Rev. Jeremiah Eames Rankin (1828-1904) featured evangelistic singing. He had already edited a book of gospel songs two years earlier, "Gospel Temperance Hymnal" having been published in 1878. Even before that, some of his original hymns had been included in "Songs of the New Life" published in 1869.

This particular Sunday night in 1880 he wanted to close the service with a farewell hymn. The only good one in the standard hymnals was John Fawcett's "Blest Be the Tie That Binds." But Rankin wanted something different, more of a lilting gospel song than a dignified stately hymn. Not finding what he wanted, and with the results of his recent study of the dictionary and the Bible in his mind, he sat down and wrote the first stanza of his own "benediction hymn":

God be with you till we meet again, By His counsels guide, uphold you;
With His sheep securely fold you; God be with you till we meet again.

He sent the words to two musicians, asking them to try their hand at composing an appropriate tune for the stanza and chorus: "Till we meet at Jesus' feet, God be with you till we meet again."

The tune that suited him and seemed to express the spirit of the words was sent in by William Gould Tomer, at that time a school teacher in Carpentersville, N.J. The music so pleased the poet that he wrote seven additional stanzas to complete his new hymn. It is interesting to note that Mr. Tomer had been at one time on the staff of General O. O. Howard, after whom the great Negro institution of higher education, Howard University, in Washington, D.C. is named. Later Dr. Rankin himself was to serve as President of this University for seven years.

Dr. John W. Bischoff, blind organist of the author's Church, revised the new tune slightly, and it was sung for the first time by the poet's Sunday night congregation in his own Church.

It is strange that a hymn so simple that of its sixteen lines eight contain the same phrase "God be with you till we meet again," should have such a hold on the affections of Christian people. But, for good or ill, it has, and, with or without the "Chorus" it is sung Sunday after Sunday as a parting hymn and as a "Christian goodbye." It was first published the year of its composition in "Gospel Bells," a collection of hymns and songs edited by the pastor, his organist and his Sunday School Superintendent.

It is fitting for an age which says "Thanks" when it means "Thank you" to be reminded that every time it says "Goodbye" it is saying a prayer, "God be with you."

15.

GOD OF OUR FATHERS, KNOWN OF OLD

When a hired girl thoughtlessly tossed the manuscript of Carlyle's "The French Revolution" into the fire, there was no one standing by to rescue it from the flames. But, fortunately for posterity, when thirty-two-year-old Rudyard Kipling cleaned out his desk and carelessly threw away a seven-stanza poem he had written on the occasion of Queen Victoria's "Diamond Jubilee," someone was present to rescue it from oblivion.

Miss Sara Norton, daughter of Harvard history professor, Charles Eliot Norton, was a guest in the Kipling home in Sussex, England, that memorable year, 1897. On the sixteenth of July, when she saw the famous author-poet gather up some papers and drop them into the waste basket, she asked permission to look through them, "just in case you are discarding something of lasting value." When Kipling consented, she examined the material and found nothing of special interest until she came across a poem which he had entitled "After." The immediate occasion which had inspired him to pen the stanzas was the pomp and ceremony attending the Lord Mayor's presentation to Her Majesty of a pearl-studded sword at Temple Bar, at the entrance to the medieval section of London during her "Jubilee" year.

"This poem is too good to throw away," the young American guest told her distinguished British host.

"I disagree," he replied, "but if you think it contains something of value, show it to Aunt Georgie (Lady Burne-Jones, a neighbor). When Aunt Georgie read the stanzas she was as enthusiastic as Sara had been. The two women encouraged Kipling to revise the poem. When he did, he reduced it from seven stanzas to five, and included the same two-line refrain after three of them; he even used Miss Norton's pen with which to make the changes. A marginal note on the completed manuscript read, "Written with Sallie's pen. R.K." Subsequently the original last line of the last stanza, "Thy mercy on thy people, Lord, Amen," was retained.

The author sent the poem to the London "Times" and it was published the very next day, July 17, 1897. The young lady who had retrieved the original was given the annotated copy by the author himself. After passing from her hands into those of relatives, it finally found its way to the British Museum, where it is now the property of the British people.

Kipling, both of whose grandfathers were Methodist preachers, showed little interest in religious matters, and never dreamed that anything he wrote would be used as a Christian hymn. "On the Road to Mandalay" and "Boots" or "The Hanging of Danny Dever" from his "Barrack Room Ballads" (1892) would hardly be used in Sunday School or Church. And while his numerous books revealed a spark of genius, they were the works of a masterful story-teller rather than a deeply spiritual writer. His friends and admirers were grieved when Queen Victoria refused to appoint him "Poet Laureate" but not surprised, for he had offended Her Majesty by calling her "The Widow of Windsor" in one of his poems. Furthermore, he had not been officially requested to furnish a paean of praise on the occasion of her "Jubilee," in accordance with established custom and tradition. But while the "official poem" has long since been forgotten, his stanzas, re-titled "The Recessional," took the country by storm. The author was praised and damned by his fellow-countrymen, some taking his warnings to heart, and others denouncing him as a traitor to his people.

As for the poet, he had written the last phrase, "Lest we forget," first, building the rest of his stanzas around those three words. He later said, "That poem gave me more trouble than anything I ever wrote. Sitting down with all my previous attempts before me, I searched through dozens of sketches until at last I found just one line I liked. That was 'Lest we forget.' Round these words 'The Recessional' was written."

Though written for a timely occasion, his lines are timeless. The mad race for power, prosperity, pomp and pleasure are not only the sins of his people in his day but the sins of every nation

49

in every age. Everyone needs to take to heart the opening lines:

God of our fathers, known of old; Lord of our far-flung battle
line,
Beneath whose awful hand we hold Dominion over palm and
pine:
Lord God of hosts, be with us yet, Lest we forget, lest we forget.

In the thirty-nine years that remained to him after he wrote these memorable words, he did not produce one line that can equal them in greatness or match them in splendor. But he did live long enough to see his beloved England accept his poem as one of its greatest literary productions.

Queen Victoria is dead, but "The Recessional" lives on!

16.

GOD MOVES IN A MYSTERIOUS WAY

"To the river, driver," ordered William Cowper as he entered the carriage.

"The river?" asked the driver, as he picked up the reins. "Where? And why?"

"Anywhere along the river bank," answered the deranged poet. "God has ordered me to take my own life, and I prefer to drown myself rather than hang myself."

"Did you say God ordered you to take your own life?" the driver asked, as he headed for the Ouse River, three miles away.

"Yes," replied the confused lawyer. "God hates me. You see I am not one of God's elect. And because I have not been elected to salvation I am to be eternally damned. And as my punishment God has ordered me to slay myself."

The driver quickly realized the unbalanced condition of his passenger's mind and breathed a prayer of thanks when a sudden fog enveloped the area. "This will help," he said to himself as he purposely lost his way in the dense fog. Several hours later he was still jogging up one road and down another, when he looked back and saw his passenger lying in a deep sleep. Stopping in front of the house where he had picked him up, the driver called, "Here we are, sir; here we are."

Roused from a deep slumber, Cowper stepped from the carriage, paid his fare, turned toward the house and said, "We're back home. How is that?"

"Got lost in the fog, sir. Sorry."

"Where did I order you to go?"

"To the river, sir, so you could take your life because you said God told you to," replied the relieved driver.

"Then God be praised for having spared me," Cowper said. "God be thanked for having over-ruled my foolish designs. I must have been in one of my melancholic moods, but I'm all right now, thanks to His great mercy." Dismissing the carriage he went into his home. That same evening in 1774, his forty-third year, reflecting upon his narrow escape from death, he wrote an autobiographical hymn which contained these majestic lines:

God moves in a mysterious way, His wonders to perform;
He plants His footsteps in the sea, And rides upon the storm.

Cowper (1731-1800) spent the last twenty-five years of his life convinced that God "was determined to betray him at every turn in this life and to torture him eternally in the next." The death of his mother when he was but six was quite a shock. Then, entering an English boarding school when still a young lad he was subjected to severe hazing and ill treatment at the hands of older boys. Because of what his biographers call "an intimate deformity" he was mauled and mistreated to such a degree that the madness which haunted his later years may be traced to this source.

At twenty-one he entered the legal profession, and was nominated for a clerkship in the British House of Lords. The strain and worry accompanying the examination for this appointment so unnerved him that he suffered the first of a series of fits of insanity. He bought poison but could not take it; he purchased a large knife but was afraid to plunge it into his heart; he hanged himself but the garter broke! There followed eighteen months in an asylum, where he suffered from the delusion that God "had it in for him" and was wreaking His vengeance upon him in a peculiar way.

At thirty-three he gained his senses long enough to experience a Christian conversion, and the consciousness of forgiven sin. A visit from a brother during his confinement to St. Alban's asylum led to his conversion, and inspired him to write "O for a closer walk with God." When his only romance terminated almost before it began, only the friendship of Rev. John Newton kept him from taking his life. The two men worked together on their "Olney Hymns" and its publication, with outstanding contributions from them both, was a landmark in the history of Christian hymnody.

The last decade of his life was plagued with more "haunting visions and strange voices" until he cried out in desperation, "Wretch! To whom death and life are alike impossible!" From his earlier years came his majestic hymns and from the lucid hours of his declining years such outstanding poems as "The Task" and "John Gilpin" as well as thousands of "eloquent cheerful letters." While he felt that God had damned him "below Judas Iscariot," the Heavenly Father, in love and tender mercy, took him back to Himself in 1800. And his hymns, written from a tortured mind and confused soul, now bring to millions of others comfort and strength such as was denied their author.

17.

HARK! THE HERALD ANGELS SING

When an Anglican clergyman turned Methodist collaborates with a Christianized Jew, something unusual is bound to happen. The Methodist preacher was Charles Wesley, a minister of the Church of England, who, with his preacher-Oxford professor brother John, were joint founders of the Methodist Church. The Jew was Felix Mendelssohn, whose father, Abraham, added "Bartholdy" to the family name, since it was his desire that his children be raised as Protestant Christians. But the collaboration was purely accidental.

By the time Charles Wesley reached his thirty-first birthday, he had had more than his share of adventure and travel. As secretary to General Oglethorpe, he had made a journey to the new colony of Georgia, remaining in the new world almost a year. He and John had returned to England with heavy and disillusioned hearts. Following John's "heart-warming" in a little prayer meeting on London's Aldersgate Street early in May, 1738, Charles had a similar experience on May 20, 1738. And from that day he sang the praise of God with fluency and power, writing more than sixty-five hundred of the noblest hymns in the English language.

In 1739, the year after he "consciously believed," he wrote a poem of some ten four-line stanzas in which he expressed his joy in the Christian faith. The first stanza read:

Hark! how all the welkin rings, "Glory to the King of Kings, Peace on earth and mercy mild, God and sinners reconciled."

In that form it was published that same year in "Hymns and Sacred Poems." Fourteen years later, George Whitfield, an associate of the Wesleys in their evangelistic labors, and one of the most powerful preachers ever to visit the Americas, took the liberty of editing Charles' hymn for a "Collection" he was planning to publish. He altered the first stanza to the form in which it is sung today: "Hark! the herald angels sing 'Glory to the newborn King.'" Further alterations by interested poets and editors polished off several more rough spots, but this Christmas hymn, in its essence still Wesley's, is perhaps the most popular English hymn in the world.

As for thirty-one-year-old Felix Mendelssohn, writing a hymn-tune was the farthest thing from his mind when he composed his "Festgesang #7" in 1840. His music was written for a celebration commemorating the anniversary of the discovery of printing. Even the great Gutenberg himself could hardly have pictured his revolutionary discovery as the inspiration for a world-famous Christmas carol. And the composer even had this to say about his music, "I think there ought to be other words to (it). If the right ones are hit I am sure that piece will be liked very much. But it will *never* do to sacred words." Doctor of Music William H. Cummings showed the German musician how wrong he was. In 1855, fifteen years after the composer had penned his work, Dr. Cummings set it to Wesley's equally famous stanzas and thus a perfect Christmas hymn was born.

While Mendelssohn considered his work a secular piece, Christians the world over compare it with passages from his sacred oratorio "Elijah" and number it among his finest sacred compositions.

The universal favor in which this magnificent hymn is held is attested by the fact that it is the only one of Charles Wesley's thousands that is included in "The Book of Common Prayer" of the Church of England. Be that as it may, it has found a lasting place in the hearts of believers the world over, who will be singing it for as many Christmases in the future as there were between the time of the birth of Jesus and the writing of the original stanzas in 1739.

18

HE LEADETH ME! O BLESSED THOUGHT!

The First Baptist Church building, on the northwest corner of Broad and Arch Streets in Philadelphia, was being torn down to make room for a modern office building to house the United Gas Improvement Company of that city. A Baptist clergyman, watching the old Church being demolished, said to a company official, "That old building has a remarkable history. A wonderful hymn, 'He Leadeth Me,' was written there." When the new structure was completed, a bronze tablet was cast and formally dedicated to the author and the occasion which inspired the writing of his best-known hymn. The inscription reads: " 'He Leadeth Me,' sung throughout the world, was written by Rev. Dr. Joseph H. Gilmore, a son of a Governor of New Hampshire, in the home of Deacon Wattson, immediately after preaching in the First Baptist Church, northwest corner Broad and Arch Streets, on the 26th day of March, 1862. The Church and Deacon Wattson's home stood on the ground upon which this building is erected. The United Gas Improvement Company, in recognition of the beauty and fame of the Hymn, and in remembrance of its distinguished author, makes this permanent record on the first day of June, 1926."

Memories harked back to that Wednesday night in March, 1862, during the dark and depressing days of the War Between the States, when a young minister was supplying the pulpit of this historic Church. Twenty-eight-year-old Rev. Joseph Henry Gilmore was well-prepared for his ministry, having graduated with honors from Brown University and Newton Theological Seminary several years before. When he and his wife moved to the "City of Brotherly Love" they little dreamed that they were embarking upon the most momentous trip of their lives. The preacher selected Psalm 23 as the Scripture for the mid-week service, and dwelt at great length on God's leadership during dark days. Over and over he repeated the words, "He leadeth me beside the still waters—He leadeth me in the paths of righteousness," and urged his listeners to follow God's leading as sheep follow the shepherd. He exhorted them to look for some cloud by day and pillar of fire by night such as God sent to lead the Hebrew children out of their Egyptian bondage into the freedom of the Promised Land.

Following the service, the visiting minister and his wife went with their hosts, Deacon and Mrs. Wattson, to the home in which they were being entertained, next-door to the downtown Church site. The pastor could not refrain from commenting again on the theme he had chosen. It haunted him, until, to get inner relief, he began to write down several stanzas on the back of a sheet of paper on which he had jotted down the notes · for his recent talk. He started with these lines:

He leadeth me! O blessed thought; O words with heavenly
    comfort fraught;
Whate'er I do, where'er I be, Still 'tis God's hand that leadeth
    me.

When he stopped, there were four stanzas and a chorus. While he promptly forgot all about his poetic version of the twenty-third Psalm, his wife didn't. She sent a copy to a Boston paper, "The Watchman and Reflector," where it was first published. William Bradbury discovered it there and set it to music, thus insuring for the author a permanent place in Christian hymnody.

While he lived to occupy many exalted positions in religious and educational circles and was the recipient of numerous well-deserved honors during his long and fruitful life of eighty-four years, Joseph Gilmore is remembered today because of a trip to Philadelphia when he was twenty-eight, four stanzas dashed off in a moment of inspiration, a wife who had sense enough to recognize a good thing when she saw it, and a composer who never let an inspiring poem get away from him.

19.

I NEED THEE EVERY HOUR

This familiar hymn, now associated with suffering and sorrow, was, in the words of the author, "wafted out to the world on the wings of love and joy." The poet, Mrs. Annie Sherwood Hawks, moved from her birthplace, Hoosick, New York to Brooklyn, and for many years was an active member of the Hanson Place Baptist Church there. About 1868 her pastor, the poet and song-writer Rev. Robert Lowry, discovered that she had unusual talent as a writer, and encouraged her to turn her poetic gifts to the production of verses for children. During his eight-year ministry there she wrote most of the poems now associated with her name. The majority of the tunes for them were composed by Dr. Lowry.

One bright morning in June, 1872, when she was thirty-seven years of age, Mrs. Hawks was busy with the usual chores that occupy the waking hours of most housewives and mothers. In the midst of daily cares and duties, she was suddenly filled with the consciousness of the nearness of her Lord.

"I wonder how anyone could live without Him," she thought, as His presence seemed to linger in the room. "How could anyone face pain or experience deep and abiding joy apart from Him?" she asked, half-aloud. "And how could they overcome temptation apart from His abiding companionship?"

The thought of her need of Christ took full possession of her, and soon, without too much effort, a series of brief couplets began forming in her mind. She could hardly wait to write them down, and soon she was penning these lines:

I need Thee every hour, Most gracious Lord; No tender voice
    like Thine, Can peace afford.
I need Thee every hour, Stay Thou near by; Temptations lose
    their power, When Thou art nigh.

Her lines were so simple she was almost ashamed to show them to her pastor. But he had insisted that she bring him every poem she wrote, so she swallowed her pride, and gave him a copy of her lyrics after Church the next Sunday morning, little dreaming that, on the wings of his music, they would sing their way into millions of hearts. Dr. Lowry read and re-read the simple stanzas until he realized that his parishioner had produced the finest bit of poetry she would every write. But, with his love of a "chorus" he felt the hymn would be incomplete without one. So when he sat down at the little organ in the living room of his Brooklyn parsonage and set Mrs. Hawks' poem to music, he added a "refrain" of his own, which read:

I need Thee, Oh, I need Thee; Every hour I need Thee;
O bless me now, my Saviour, I come to Thee,

This wasn't the first time Dr. Lowry had written a "chorus." He admired Isaac Watts' great hymn, "Come we that love the Lord," so much that he felt it deserved a more lyrical melody than the stately cadences of "St. Thomas" to which it was sung. So he composed a tune all his own, adding a "chorus" which contained these words:

We're marching to Zion, Beautiful, beautiful Zion;
We're marching upward to Zion, The beautiful city of God.

And as much as he admired Wesley's majestic Easter hymn, "Christ the Lord Is Risen Today, Alleluia," he could not rest until he had written and composed one of his own, "chorus" and all. It is the perennial favorite "Christ Arose," which is sung by adults as well as children the world over at Eastertide.

The new song, "I Need Thee Every Hour," was sung for the first time at the National Baptist Sunday School Association meeting in Cincinnati, Ohio, in November 1872. The following year it was included in a new songbook, "Royal Diadem" compiled by Dr. Lowry and W. H. Doane.

Years later the author said, "My poem was prophetic rather than expressive of my own experience, and I do not understand why it so touched the great throbbing heart of humanity. It was not until long years after, when the shadow of a great loss fell over my way, that I understood something of the comforting in the words I had been permitted to write in my hours of sweet security and peace."

Following the death of her husband in 1888, Mrs. Hawks made her home with one of her three children in Bennington, Vermont, until her death in 1918, at the age of eighty-three.

20

IN THE CROSS OF CHRIST I GLORY

It is hard to believe that the author of this hymn was called "the most unpopular governor Hong Kong ever had!" It is well nigh incredible that he, Sir John Bowring (1792-1872) by his high-handed and insolent policies in that Crown Colony actually brought on the second Opium War between Great Britain and China, 1856-1858. But the facts of history cannot be denied. The explanation may lie in the change wrought in an idealistic youth who wrote his splendid hymns before he was thirty-five, and then, corrupted by power, became the hardhearted politician, "full of conceit, without any very clear idea of political principles on a large scale."

He was so hated that an attempt was made to kill him and the entire British garrison at Hong Kong by putting arsenic in the bread. While his health was seriously impaired by this act, Lady Bowring died from its effects. To his credit let it be remembered that he was one of the most brilliant and versatile men England has ever produced. He could speak fluently in twenty-two languages and converse in almost a hundred more; he served his King as "minister plenipotentiary and envoy extraordinary" in posts all over the world. Deserved honors were heaped upon him in his old age, although the facts of his life and influence could not be discounted.

During his youthful days, he felt the call to preach and had a strong desire to enter the ministry of the Unitarian Church, but was dissuaded from this course by his father who had "higher" ambitions for his son. He wrote in 1820, "It will be the height of my ambition to do something which may connect my work with the literature of the age." This was realized when, at thirty-three, in 1825, inspired by the words of St.

Paul in Galatians 6:14, "Far be it from me to glory save in the cross of our Lord Jesus Christ," he wrote a hymn which began:

In the cross of Christ I glory, Towering o'er the wrecks of time; All the light of sacred story, Gathers round its head sublime.

It was not until twenty-four years later that he saw the ruins of a cathedral in Macao in China, over which a cross was still standing, which some claimed as the inspiration for his hymn. But that same year, 1825, he wrote, "God Is Love, His Mercy Brightens" and the stirring missionary hymn, "Watchman, Tell Us of the Night." Author of more than thirty-six volumes, a distinguished member of Parliament, knighted by Queen Victoria, he died at Exeter, England in 1872, his eightieth year.

His words may never have achieved their deserved popularity had it not been for a rainy Sunday morning in 1849. Ithamar Conkey was organist and choir director at Central Baptist Church, Norwich, Connecticut, that year, and his minister, Rev. Dr. Hiscox, was preaching a series of sermons on "The Words on the Cross." The thirty-four-year-old musician was grieved when he went to the choir room to rehearse the anthem that particular Sunday just before the Morning Worship Service. To his dismay only one soprano showed up. As if that were not bad enough, not a single alto, tenor or bass put in an appearance. He was so disgusted and discouraged that after he played the prelude that morning he cut off the organ motor, closed the console, locked it, and went home, leaving the minister to carry on as best he could under the circumstances. Since the organ and choir loft were in the balcony at the rear of the Church, he could leave without attracting the attention of the congregation.

That afternoon Conkey tried to raise his spirits by playing the piano. As he sat at the keyboard, he thought of his minister and the series of sermons he was delivering on Jesus' Seven Last Words. The stanzas of "In the Cross of Christ I Glory," which the pastor had quoted, came into his mind, and right then and there he composed the hymn tune to which they are now universally sung. He confessed later that "the inspiration that came to me at that moment was a vivid contrast to my feelings at the morning service."

62

Mrs. B. H. Rathbun, his twenty-four-year-old leading soprano, was, with her husband, a faithful member of the choir. As a compliment to her, since she was the only singer who showed up that rainy Sunday morning, he named his new tune "Rathbun." She died five years later, at twenty-nine. Mr. Conkey moved to New York City and served as bass soloist and conductor of the quartet-choir at the Madison Avenue Baptist Church until his death in 1867.

So, from the pen of a disillusioned politician and a disappointed organist and choir-master, came the stirring strains of "In the Cross of Christ I Glory," which breathe the air of confidence and conviction, and spread the message of joy and hope to all the world.

21

INTO THE WOODS MY MASTER WENT

Some men make a bold attempt to write hymns in the hopes that one or two will achieve immortality. Others write for the sheer joy of writing, with no thought of creating something that future generations will take to their hearts. To their surprise and amazement, some stray bit of verse dashed off in an inspired moment meets a deep human need and wings its way into the hymnals of the Church.

Thus it was with the versatile southern poet, Georgia-born Sidney Lanier, one of the rare southerners who made a permanent contribution to ecumenical hymnody. In his brief life of thirty-nine years he wrote fourteen volumes of prose and at least ten books of poetry, a remarkable record in view of his weak physical body and his lifelong struggle against poverty, disease and disappointment.

When he wrote his wife, "Let my name perish—the poetry is good poetry . . . and the heart that needs it will find it," little did he dream that many hearts would find solace and strength in sixteen lines entitled "The Ballad of the Trees and the Master," which he wrote the year before his untimely death.

Life was not all bitterness to Lanier, but he seemed to have had more than his rightful share. A self-taught scholar who entered college at fourteen, his education was interrupted by the Civil War, in which conflict he was at various times a scout, a signal officer, a blockade runner and a prisoner. His physical breakdown dated from his prison hardships and privations. Following the war he traveled widely and tried to earn a living at such varied jobs at a hotel clerk, school teacher, lawyer and writer. But even then happiness and contentment were denied him. So he began the serious study of music which had been one of his first loves. He perfected this talent to such a degree that, despite the threat of tuberculosis that hung over him for many years, he became the outstanding flutist in the country, and an accomplished violinist as well. From Texas he went to Baltimore where he played in the Peabody Orchestra and lectured on English Literature at Johns Hopkins.

But the ravages of disease wore him down, until he had to leave the city to seek solace in the mountains of western North Carolina. There, as his own life slowly ebbed away, he thought of the death of Jesus centuries before. Like the Master, who spent many lonely hours on Mount Olivet prior to his betrayal and crucifixion, Lanier often went into the woods to regain composure and find inner peace. When he could no longer play his prized flute, one of his most valued possessions, and when no more did the applause of the multitudes ring in his ears as it had at the close of many a successful concert, and when almost nothing could be done for him that had not already been done, he penned his sixteen lines that began:

Into the woods my Master went, Clean forspent, forspent.

He died the very next year, 1881, in Tryon, N.C. unaware of the fact that future generations would look back upon him as one of the leading hymn writers of the southern states.

William Steffe, author of the hymn "Say, brothers, will you meet us, On Canaan's happy shore" was a Richmonder who wrote his song in Georgia. It is to his melody that we now sing "The Battle Hymn of the Republic." Lowell Mason, the father of American hymnology and public school music, long a resident of Boston, was at one time a bank clerk in Savannah, Georgia. It was while he lived in the south that he composed his hymn tune for "From Greenland's Icy Mountains." And Charles Wesley himself must have sung some of his great hymns beneath the famed Wesley Oaks on St. Simon's Island, near Brunswick, Georgia during his brief stay in the Colonies. But when we think of American composers and hymn writers, we include such "northerners" as Fosdick, North, Merrill, Holmes, S. F. Smith, Palmer, Stebbins, Bradbury, Bliss, Root, Lowry, Sankey and others.

But few wrote as exquisitely or as beautifully in the brief space of sixteen lines as did the south's leading poet, Sidney Lanier.

22.

IT IS WELL WITH MY SOUL

Tragedy preceded the writing of the words of this hymn and followed closely the composing of the music.

The French liner, "S.S. Ville du Havre," was the most luxurious ship afloat when it sailed from New York in November, 1873. Among her passengers was Mrs. H. G. Spafford of Chicago, making the trip with her four children, Maggie, Tanetta, Annie and Bessie. Mr. Spafford was unable to make the voyage with his family because of business commitments in Chicago, so recently ravaged by the Great Fire. But, even though he was happy that his family was travelling on a ship with Christian companions, some last-minute premonition made him change the cabin they occupied to one toward the bow of the vessel. He told them "Goodbye," promising to meet them in France in a few weeks.

At two o'clock on the morning of November 22, 1873, when the luxury liner was several days out, and sailing on a quiet sea, she was rammed by the English iron sailing vessel, the "Lochearn." In two hours the "Ville du Havre," one of the largest ships afloat, settled to the bottom of the ocean, with a loss of some two-hundred twenty-six lives, including the four Spafford children. Nine days later when the survivors landed at Cardiff, Wales, Mrs. Spafford cabled her husband these two words, "Saved alone." When he received her message, he said to a dear friend, "I am glad to trust the Lord when it will cost me something." For him it was a second time of testing, coming almost too soon upon the heels of the first. In the Chicago Fire he had lost everything he owned; in the tragedy at sea he had lost his four precious children. As soon as he could, he booked passage on a ship to Europe to join his wife. On the way over, in December of that same year, 1873, the Captain called him into his cabin and said, "I believe we are now passing over the place where the 'Ville du Havre' went down."

That night he found it hard to sleep. But faith soon conquered doubt, and there, in the mid-Atlantic, out of his heart-break and pain, Mr. Spafford wrote five stanzas, the first of which contained these lines:

When peace like a river attendeth my way, When sorrows like
    sea-billows roll,
Whatever my lot, Thou hast taught me to say, "It is well, it is
    well with my soul!"

When they met some weeks later, Mrs. Spafford said, "I have not lost my children. We are only separated for a little time."

Mr. Spafford and Philip Paul Bliss, song leader and composer, were not strangers. Both had been associated with Moody and Sankey in several of their evangelistic campaigns, and Bliss had led the singing on a few occasions when Mr. Spafford had been the speaker. At the request of the author, Bliss agreed to set Spafford's poem to music. On the last Friday in November, 1876, in a meeting in Farwell Hall, Chicago, where more than a thousand ministers were gathered, Bliss introduced "It Is Well with my Soul" as a sacred solo. A month later, when the ink on the manuscript paper was hardly dry, Mr. and Mrs. Bliss, leaving their two children with his mother, took a train from Buffalo, N.Y. enroute to Chicago, where a new series of services was scheduled to begin shortly after New Year's Day. They left Buffalo on Friday afternoon, December 29, 1876. At eight o'clock that night, while approaching Ashtabula, Ohio, a bridge crossing a ravine gave way and the train and its seven cars of passengers plunged into the icy river below. Fire broke out almost immediately, killing many who had escaped drowning, but were imprisoned by falling beams and twisted timbers. Of the one-hundred-sixty passengers, just fifty-nine bodies were eventually accounted for; there were only fourteen survivors. One of them reported that Bliss could have escaped, but, as his wife was hopelessly caught in the wreckage, he remained at her side, and together they met the onrushing flames and certain death. For three days his friends remained at the scene of the disaster, but they found nothing that could be identified with the thirty-eight-year-old song leader or his wife, although scores of articles were raked from the ashes and gathered from the bottom of the river.

They have no earthly grave—the four Spafford children who drowned in the middle of the Atlantic Ocean, and Mr. and Mrs. Bliss who perished in the train wreck in Ohio. But their hymn, which followed one tragedy and preceded another, lives forever in the hearts of Christian people, who rejoice that both the Spaffords and the Blisses could truthfully and triumphantly say,

"It is well, it is well with my soul."

23.

JESUS CALLS US

Few ministers' wives can write a hymn to order for their husbands, even if they are famous poets in their own right. But Cecil Frances Alexander did just that for her preacher husband, and, while the sermon that preceded it has long since been forgotten, her poem has found a lasting place in the hearts of the Church universal.

It began long before her marrige to Rev. William Alexander, future Archbishop of Armagh and Primate of all Ireland. Because, when she was still twenty-one-year-old Cecil Humphreys, she had been so profoundly influenced by Rev. John Keble's book, "The Christian Year" that her first book, "Verses for Holy Seasons" was actually a "Christian Year" for children, containing a hymn or poem for each Sunday of the year with additional verses for special occasions.

In one of her Sunday School classes, some of her pupils asked, "Miss Humphreys, what do the words in the Apostles' Creed mean?" She tried to explain to them in their own language the deeper meaning behind each of the phrases of the Creed. Later she decided to reduce her teachings to poetic form and soon her boys and girls were singing about the Creed as well as studying it. For the first phrase, "I believe in God the Father Almighty," she wrote her hymn "All things bright and beautiful"; for "born of the Virgin Mary" she wrote, "Once in Royal David's City"; and to explain the meaning of the death of Jesus who was "crucified, dead and buried" she wrote "There is a Green Hill Far Away." In 1848, the year of her marriage, she published her book, "Hymns for Little Children," which included the ones inspired by the Creed.

One afternoon during the week of November 25, 1852, her twenty-ninth year, she sat alone in the living room of their parsonage in Tyrone, Ireland, working over a new poem. When her husband came home he found her busily revising her latest work.

"And what is the effort of this afternoon about, my dear?" he asked, jokingly. She chided him for his sarcasm, and then replied, "It is a new poem based on your sermon of last Sunday morning." He looked surprised and said, "Honestly, dear, I didn't think you were paying attention. But it does help a preacher to know he has at least one sympathetic listener in his congregation, even if it is only his wife." She reminded him that he had preached on "The burial of Moses," which was the subject of her new poem. When she handed him the papers over which she had been working, he began to read one of the most magnificent poems in the English language:

By Nebo's lonely mountain, On this side Jordan's wave,
In a vale in the land of Moab, There lies a lonely grave.
But no man built that sepulchre, And no man saw it e'er;
For the angels of God upturned the sod, And laid the dead
　　　man there.

When he finished the last stanza he turned and said seriously, "My dear, I salute you. This is the noblest piece of poetry you have ever written. Who knows but the day may come when I shall enjoy the distinction of being pointed out as the husband of Mrs. Cecil Humphreys Alexander."

Later that evening, as they talked about the sermon and the poem it had inspired, Mr. Alexander said, "Next Sunday is St. Andrew's Day. Since you wrote about the burial of Moses *after* last Sunday's sermon, I wonder if you could write a poem for next Sunday morning *before* you hear the sermon." "I'll do what I can," she told him.

He took down the Bible and read the account of the calling of Andrew by Jesus as recorded in Mark 1:16-18. They discussed the coming sermon during supper, and she promised to do her best with the poem he had requested. That night, before retiring, she read the familiar Scripture verses again, and soon wrote down the stanzas which he was to read at the close of his sermon the following Sunday morning. Her first stanza contained these lines:

Jesus calls us, o'er the tumult, Of our life's wild, restless sea;
Day by day His sweet voice soundeth, Saying, "Christian, follow
me!"

Before her death in 1895, she had written more than four-
hundred hymns and poems. Over a quarter of a million copies
of "Hymns for Little Children" were sold. But nothing she wrote
ever received the universal acclaim that has greeted the hymn she
prepared for her husband to use in his sermon on St. Andrew's
Day in 1852.

24

JUST AS I AM, WITHOUT ONE PLEA

Charlotte Elliott was mad at herself, her family and God. At thirty-three, when she should have been enjoying radiant health, she had become an invalid because of the strain of a musical and artistic education.

"If God loved me," she complained, "He would not have treated me this way. He would have dealt with me as I would deal with my brother and sister, or any other person I claimed to love."

This rebellious spirit not only poisoned her heart but put a strain on the life of the entire family. It was to try to mellow the soul of his talented daughter that her father, Mr. Charles Elliott, invited Dr. Cesar Malan, noted Swiss minister and musician, to be a guest in their home at Westfield Lodge, Brighton, England, in May, 1822. Malan, "the greatest name in the history of French hymnology," was seated at the dinner table with members of the Elliott family on May 9 when Charlotte gave vent to one of her typical emotional outbursts, condemning God for His cruelty to her, and criticizing her brother, Rev. Henry Venn Elliott, as well as her sister and father for their lack of sympathy. Her father, embarrassed at her lack of respect for their distinguished guest, excused himself and left the room with his son and second daughter.

Dr. Malan and Charlotte faced each other across the table. After a few tense moments of silence, he said, "You are tired of yourself, aren't you?"

"What do you mean?" she asked, angrily.

"You are holding to your hate and anger because you have nothing else in the world to cling to," he replied. "Consequently, you have become sour, bitter and resentful."

"What is your cure?" she asked.

He said, "You need the faith you are trying to despise."

Sensing an understanding heart, Charlotte soon unburdened

herself, releasing the pent-up feelings she had been struggling to conceal for many years. Dr. Malan explained how God, as we know Him in Jesus, could help her find peace for her soul as well as her mind and body. Suddenly she saw herself as God knew her and was ashamed.

"Dr. Malan," she said, "I want to apologize for my disrespectful behavior during dinner and I want to ask your forgiveness. Also I want your advice. If I wanted to become a Christian and to share the peace and joy you possess, what would I do? How would I go about it?"

"You would give yourself to God just as you are now," he explained, "with your fightings and fears, hates and loves, jealousies and quick temper, pride and shame, and He would take them from you in proportion to faith, and put His great love in their place."

"Just as you are now," she repeated, and then added, "I would come to God just as I am. Is that right?"

"Exactly," he replied, "praying this prayer, 'O God, I come to you just as I am, to be made over by you and to be used by you for your glory and your Kingdom.' "

Fourteen years later, on the anniversary of that conversation, Charlotte, soon to be lovingly called "The Sunbeam of Brighton," received her annual letter from Dr. Malan. Reminiscing over the events of that meeting, and the wonderful change that had come over her life, she recalled his words, "Come just as you are," and her reply, "Just as I am, I come." While her brother and sister were away from home assisting in a bazaar for the benefit of St. Mary's school, Charlotte, now forty-seven, penned her spiritual autobiography in a seven-stanza poem which began:

Just as I am, without one plea, But that thy blood was shed for me,
And that thou bidd'st me come to thee, O Lamb of God, I come.

Her brother later remarked, "In all my preaching I have not done so much good as my sister has been permitted to accomplish by her one hymn 'Just as I Am.' "

She passed away at Brighton in her eighty-second year, in 1871, "in the full hope and triumph of the Gospel she had sung so long."

25.

LEAD KINDLY LIGHT

St. Paul was stopped in his tracks by the blinding light of the sun on the Damascus road, but it was the kindly light of a star that led the Wise Men to the manger of the Christ child. Since then, many have sought to guide their footsteps by the radiance of the noonday sun, when God has been seeking to order their ways by the gentler glow of an evening star. So it was with brilliant thirty-two-year-old Anglican clergyman, John Henry Newman. Returning to his native England from an extended visit to Rome, he boarded an Italian orange-boat for the journey to Marseilles, France, accompanied by a brother minister and his personal servant. Newman, deeply hurt because of the lack of religious vitality in the Church of England, was anxious to revitalize the dying devotion of her ministers and members. His visit to Italy had been made with the express purpose of discussing his spiritual condition as well as that of the Church of his choice with leaders of the Roman Catholic Church. Now, enroute home, he was more confused than ever. Day after day he prayed for a sign that would assure him that he had not been overlooked by Divine Providence. Now, to make matters worse, the orange-boat is becalmed in the Straits of Bonifacio, between the islands of Corsica and Sardinia, in the Mediterranean Sea. It is late afternoon, Sunday, June 16, 1833.

The restless minister paces the deck and calls to God to send a wind so the ship can get under way. His friend tries to reason with him, but to no avail. The distressed minister cannot be so easily quieted. Since there is no calm in his troubled heart, why should not the elements of nature themselves be as turbulent. "Maybe God is trying to calm you," his friend suggests, "by sending this deadening calm over the sea." But Newman will have none of that. Turning to the captain, who is supervising the shifting of orange crates to keep the fruit from spoiling beneath the hot sun, the distraught clergyman cries out, "Captain, when do we sail?" "We are more anxious to sail than you, sir," he replies. "A few more days in this sun and our fruit will rot." "Isn't there something you can do?" Newman asks, still pacing up and down the deck. The captain continues working as he answers, "One step at a time, young man; one step at a time. We who sail before the wind have learned to wait for the wind." Newman senses a mild rebuke in those words and mutters to himself, "One step at a time. I want to leap, not step." Looking at the captain, he shouts, "Call down a wind, captain!" The captain remains unperturbed. "Am I so proud as to defy God, and demand that He loose His winds for my benefit alone?" he replies. "Pride does not rule my will, sir. I cannot choose my path. He who handles the winds and sends them on their appointed courses to do His bidding and to obey His will, will breathe across the waters in His own good time, and cause them to tremble and be alive again—and not until then do we sail."

The hot, humid day finally gives way to the long, sticky night. When the captain comes on deck he sees the two clergymen still walking up and down. Turning to them, he points heavenward and says, "The star is shining again. If a wind rises tonight, the sails can catch the breeze and we can chart our course safely to our desired haven." Newman asks, "By that one little star?" The captain replies, "One needs the sun in the day but one little star is sufficient at night," and returns to his cabin. Newman stares at his friend. "The star—the star!! I've been looking for a sun to be my guide, and God has sent me a star. I was expecting the brilliant light of noonday to reveal God's entire plan for my life, but He sent the kindly light of a star to show me the way, one step at a time." His mood suddenly changes. "I know now why God dropped me here, to teach me this lesson. I see it clearly now. I was blind before." In the inspiration of that moment and the glow of that experience, Newman wrote his greatest hymn. In three stanzas, he told of his spiritual pilgrimage from doubt to faith, from confusion to certainty. The hymn began with these lines:

Lead, kindly light! amid the encircling gloom; Lead Thou me
    on.
The night is dark and I am far from home; Lead Thou me on!
Keep Thou my feet; I do not ask to see
The distant scene. One step enough for me.

Twelve years after he wrote these majestic words, he forsook
the Church of England and united with the Roman Catholic
Church. The honors that were heaped upon him were climaxed
when Pope Leo XIII made him a Cardinal in 1879, ending what
Newman called "a period in which I lived a lonely, disappointed life." He died in his eighty-ninth year, in Birmingham,
England, August 11, 1890, "a great Englishman and a great
saint."

26.

LEAD ON O KING ETERNAL

Forty-two years after Henry Smart wrote a hymn tune in England, a member of the graduating class of an American Theological Seminary wrote a commencement hymn. The two, written so many years and so many miles apart, now constitute one of the finest hymns of the Church militant. A more perfect wedding of words and music would be hard to find!

Henry Smart, one of England's finest organists, composers and organ-designers, was associated with the Parish Church, Blackburn, Lancashire, England, from 1831 to 1836. English Reformation Day is celebrated annually on October 4th. For the three-hundredth anniversary of this glorious event, October 4, 1835, a great musical festival was scheduled to be held at Blackburn and the twenty-two-year-old organist was asked to write a new hymn tune for the occasion.

"If it meets with the approval of the people, I will name it 'Lancashire,' he said, and sat down to compose a thrilling new tune for Reginald Heber's stanzas, "From Greenland's Icy Mountains." The result was a tune that is in higher favor now than when it was composed over a century ago. It bears the name the musician selected for it before he composed it.

The last fifteen years of his life, Smart was totally blind. But he continued to serve as organist at St. Pancras Church, London, until his death, because of his remarkable musical memory. In addition to "Lancashire," he is remembered for the tunes "Regent Square" (Angels from the Realms of Glory) and "Pilgrims" (Hark, Hark, My Soul, Angelic Songs Are Swelling). Among blind hymn writers are such outstanding poets as Rev. George Matheson, Fanny Crosby and John Milton; and numbered with the blind composer is American-born Adam Geibel, who wrote such tunes as "Geibel" (a new tune for "Stand

Up for Jesus") and the popular quartet favorite "Kentucky Babe."

Most class poems in high school and college are printed in the "Annual" as a matter of courtesy. There they live their brief day and as suddenly die! But when the graduating class of 1888 at Andover Theological Seminary made commencement plans, the leaders turned to classmate Ernest W. Shurtleff (1862-1917) and said, "Ernest, you write the class poem. After all, you have already published two volumes of poetry and what's the use of having a distinguished author in the class if he cannot rise to the occasion and do his class the honor of writing an original poem just for them!"

The twenty-six-year-old future Congregational minister replied, "I don't know whether to ask for congratulations or condolences. But what kind of a poem do you want?"

A classmate spoke up, "Not the usual kind of sentimental slush associated with graduations. We have had enough of that in high school and college."

"Make up your minds," young Shurtleff urged. "Do you want a poem or a hymn?"

"Make it a hymn," his classmates said enthusiastically. "And write it so we can sing it to a familiar tune," they added.

"What tune, for example?" the poet asked.

The others discussed several tunes which were popular with the student body but finally concluded that Henry Smart's tune "Lancashire," to which they sang Heber's missionary hymn, was their favorite.

"Then our graduation hymn must be a militant marching song," Shurtleff said. "We've been spending our days of preparation here. Now the day of march has come and we go out to follow the leadership of the King of Kings, to conquer the world under His banner. Without the roll of drums or the clashing of swords, we can 'fight the good fight of faith,' and with our deeds of love and mercy subdue the kingdoms of this world for the Kingdom of our Lord!"

With those ideas ringing in his ears, the young man went to his room and wrote the hymn for his graduating class, to be sung to the tune they loved above all others. A few days later the young ministers joined in singing for the first time the new hymn, which began:

Lead on, O King Eternal, The day of march has come,
Henceforth in fields of conquest, Thy tents shall be our home;
Through days of preparation, Thy grace has made us strong,
And now, O King Eternal, We lift our battle song.

With the strains of that hymn in their hearts, the young preachers left the ivied halls of the seminary to battle for God against the foes of righteousness, determined to be "faithful unto death."

The author, after filling pulpits in Churches of his denomination in several states, went abroad to perform the crowning work of his life. In 1895 he founded the American Church in Frankfort, Germany, and from 1906 until his death in 1917 he worked with student activities in Paris. For him as for all young ministers "the crown awaits the conquest" and their cry is always "Lead on, O God of might."

27.

LET THE LOWER LIGHTS BE BURNING

Philip Paul Bliss (1838-1876) had two rare gifts: he was about as ecumenical as a Christian can be, and he could rarely hear a good story without being inspired to write a new song.

When he was twelve years old he was immersed into the fellowship of the Baptist Church, Cherry Flats, Tioga County, Pennsylvania, but not long thereafter he began to participate in Methodist camp meetings and revival services. When he married, he united with the Presbyterian Church of which his wife was an active member; and for some years he was Sunday School Superintendent and Choir Member of the First Congregational Church, Chicago.

As for his musical training, it was hit-or-miss for many years because of his poverty. When he heard a piano for the first time, he was a ten-year-old barefoot boy. He was so fascinated by the music that he entered the house and said to the young lady who was playing, "O lady, play some more." Instead of responding courteously, she rebuked him for coming into her home barefooted and sent him speedily on his way. Later he was associated with song-writer George F. Root and for nearly ten years conducted singing schools, musical institutes and conventions throughout western United States. He had been about everything from a farm worker to a sawmill operator to an assistant cook in a lumber camp by the time he was converted, but he gladly and enthusiastically gave the rest of his life to the singing of the praise of God and the writing of songs expressive of his own religious experience.

Later when royalties from his "Gospel Songs" poured in to the amount of thirty-thousand dollars, despite his own financial condition he turned over the entire amount to his friend and co-worker, Major Whittle, for the furtherance of their evangelistic efforts.

One night he was listening closely as Dwight L. Moody was preaching. The eloquent minister told a story concerning the captain of a boat that was nearing the Cleveland harbor on a dark and stormy night. Added to the dangers from wild winds and mountainous waves was the further hazard of trying to approach the harbor when not a single star could be seen in the blackened sky. The captain, seeing but one light from a lighthouse, asked the pilot, "Are you sure this is Cleveland?" "Quite sure," the pilot replied. "Where are the lower lights?" he asked again. "Gone out, sir," the pilot answered. "Can you make the harbor?" he asked a third time. "We must or we perish, sir!!" was the reply. Despite the strong hand and brave heart of the man at the wheel, in the darkness he missed the channel and the vessel crashed upon the rocks with great loss of life. Moody concluded with this exhortation, "The Master will take care of the great lighthouse; let us keep the lower lights burning."

That very night, Bliss wrote the words and music of one of his most popular gospel songs:

Brightly beams our Father's mercy, From His lighthouse evermore;
But to us He gives the keeping Of the lights along the shore.
Let the lower lights be burning, Send a gleam across the wave;
Some poor fainting, struggling seaman, You may rescue, you may save.

The song was first published in "Gospel Songs" in 1874, two years before Bliss' tragic and untimely death.

This was not the first time such an inspiration had hit him. Three years earlier he had heard Rev. Mr. Brundage close a sermon with these words, "He who is almost persuaded is almost saved, but to be almost saved is to be entirely lost." With that sentence ringing in his ears, he wrote the words and music of "Almost Persuaded." When a minister spoke of Daniel's bravery in opening his windows toward Jerusalem and praying, despite an edict of the King forbidding such an act, he wrote both

"Dare to Be a Daniel" and "Are Your Windows Open Toward Jerusalem." From the Old Testament story of Jonathan and his armour-bearer winning an unexpected victory over the enemy, he composed "Only an Armour-Bearer." The newspaper account of a group of soldiers being surrounded on a hilltop during the Civil War, calling upon their fellows to rescue them from the enemy, only to receive this reply from their commanding officer, "Hold the fort! I'm coming!" led him to write one of his most rousing songs, "Hold the Fort!!"

Gifted with a remarkable voice, ranging from low D flat to high A flat, he introduced many of his compositions himself. From his fluent pen flowed such familiar favorites as "The Light of the World Is Jesus," "I Am So Glad that Jesus Loves Me," "Man of Sorrows, What a Name," "More Holiness Give Me," "Wonderful Words of Life," "I Will Sing of My Redeemer," and "Pull for the Shore." During the twelve years from 1864, when he published his first song, a popular ballad, "Lora Vale," until his death in 1876, he made a deep, profound and abiding impression upon the musical life of American Christendom. While some of his compositions are not as popular now as when they were written, others have found a place worthy of their lasting beauty in the hymnals and hearts of Christians throughout the world.

The story of his accidental death is told in connection with the hymn for which he composed the music, "It Is Well with My Soul."

28

MASTER THE TEMPEST IS RAGING

"God does not care for me or mine," said Mary Ann Baker, rebelliously. "This particular manifestation of what they call 'divine providence' is unworthy of a God of love."

Word had just come from the south that her beloved brother had passed away after suffering many months from a long and lingering illness. She described him as "a young man of rare loveliness and promise of character." Victim of the same disease that had already claimed the lives of his father and mother, young Baker left Chicago and traveled a thousand miles from home in the fruitless search for a climate that would heal better than the cold damp winters to which he was accustomed. But his condition grew worse instead of better, and adding to his misery, was the fact that his favorite sister was bedridden herself back home in Chicago and could not come to look after him in his final, fatal illness. For two long weeks telegraph wires carried messages back and forth between brother and sister, before the last telegram came, telling of his death.

"I have always tried to believe on Christ and give the Master a consecrated life," she said, "but this is more than I can bear. What have I done to deserve this? What have I left undone that God should wreak His vengeance upon me in this way?"

But, as the weeks passed, God Himself as she learned to know more of Him through Jesus, began to still the tempest in what she called her "unsanctified heart." Gradually she came to realize that God is always a loving Father, whether we are well or sick, rich or poor, and whether we succeed or fail, live or die. A deeper, richer faith and more sincere trust took possession of her, and began to transform her from a rebellious daughter into an obedient and loving child.

It was at this time, in 1874, that Rev. H. R. Palmer asked her to write several songs on the Sunday School lessons for that particular year. The theme for one of the Sundays was "Christ Stilling the Tempest." The Scripture lesson was taken from Mark 4:37-39, and contained these familiar words, "And he arose and rebuked the wind and said unto the sea, Peace, be still. And the wind ceased and there was a great calm."

She hesitated to try to express the majesty of that scene in an original poem since it had been done so superbly more than fourteen-hundred years before by St. Anatolius. A translation of his hymn was found in many hymnals. It began with these lines:

> Fierce was the wild billow, Dark was the night;
> Oars labored heavily, Foam glimmered white.
> Trembled the mariners, Peril was nigh;
> Then saith the God of God, "Peace! It is I!"

But out of her own experience of tragedy she had learned that oftentimes Christ stills the troubled heart rather than, or as much as, the troubled sea, and that possibly the miracle of Jesus had changed the frightened disciples as much as the elements of nature. That had been the case with her. And with that in mind she began to write:

Master, the tempest is raging, The billows are tossing high;
The sky is o'er shadowed with blackness, No shelter or help is nigh.
Carest thou not that we perish? How canst thou lie asleep,
When each moment so madly is threat'ning, A grave in the angry deep?

When she finished, she had three stanzas and a chorus, for which Dr. Palmer himself composed the music that very same year.

The hymn was first published in "Songs of Love for the Bible School" but it did not achieve its deserved popularity until seven years later. James A. Garfield had been President of the United States just four months when he left The White House enroute to his college class reunion at Williams College, in 1881. A disappointed office-seeker, Charles Guiteau, struck him down with an assassin's bullet as he was walking to his train through the station in Washington, D.C. For weeks he hovered between life and death, finally passing away September 19, 1881. During these trying weeks, people re-discovered "Master the Tempest Is Raging" and Christians throughout the country sang it over and over again as they prayed for the life of their President. From that time on it was printed and reprinted in songbooks and hymnals and won for itself a permanent place in the life of the Church.

The author "grew in grace and in the knowledge of our Lord and Saviour Jesus Christ" until she could truthfully say, in vivid contrast to the bitterness of her rebellious years, "God's way is the best."

29.

MORE LOVE TO THEE, O CHRIST

"Why should this happen to us, of all people?" asked Mrs. Elizabeth Prentiss of her minister husband, as the tears flowed down her cheeks.

"Maybe we should ask ourselves why a thing like this should *not* happen to us? Are we better than any of the other families who have lost loved ones in this epidemic?" he asked, sympathetically. "Does God owe us a special favor that He does not owe any other family? Or does He play favorites with anyone?"

Mrs. Prentiss dropped her face in her hands and wept for a long time until she felt she had no more tears to shed. She thought of all she had done up to that time when death had come, suddenly and swiftly, to claim her loved ones. Born in Portland, Maine, the daughter of a devout clergyman, she had early displayed unusual literary talent. When a young girl of sixteen she was a regular contributor to one of the nation's leading magazines, "The Youth's Companion," published in Boston. After completing her education she had taught school for several years. At twenty-seven she became the bride of Rev. George L. Prentiss, and moved to New York City where he was pastor of the Mercer Street Presbyterian Church.

It was after eleven years of marriage, in 1856, that tragedy struck and took away the precious loved ones from the family circle. For weeks she was almost inconsolable, despite the sincerity of her Christian faith and her firm belief in the fatherhood of God. The members of their congregation were as loving and considerate as they could be, ministering to the pastor and his wife during the days of their sorrow, taking care of the house, fixing the meals and generally supervising the day-by-day affairs of the household.

"George," she said one evening when they had returned home from the cemetery, " 'The night is dark and I am far from home.' What are we to do now? Just sit silently, passively by while our home is broken up, our lives wrecked, our hopes shattered, our dreams dissolved?"

Her husband replied, lovingly, "This is our opportunity to show forth in our lives that which we have been preaching and teaching and believing together for so many years."

"Sometimes I don't think I can stand living for another moment, much less a lifetime," she added.

"But it is in times like these that God loves us all the more, just as we love our own children more when they are sick or troubled or in distress," he continued. "Jesus said, 'In the world you have tribulation, but be of good cheer—have courage—I have overcome the world.' Suffering is not sent by God as a disciplinary measure; nor is it here to be argued over, rationalized, discussed or philosophized upon. It is here to be used and mastered for His glory."

After a few minutes of heavy silence, Mrs. Prentiss looked up and said, "I remember so well one phrase you used in last Sunday's sermon. It has helped me very much during these trying days."

"What was that?" he asked.

"You said several times, 'Love can keep the soul from going blind.' "

"And it is true, my dear. The more we love God as we know Him in Jesus, the more His healing miracle takes place in our own hearts. The less we love Him, the less chance there is that we will be able to stand the agony and pain of our loss."

When he went out to make several pastoral calls before supper, she sat in the living room, thumbing through the Bible, reading several selections, some silently to herself, and some aloud so the sound of her voice would bolster her faith. Then, laying the Book down, she looked through a hymnal, seeking light and consolation from the hymns which reflected the sorrows and triumphs of other Christians in similar circumstances. When she came across "Nearer My God to Thee," she read it aloud several times, praying in her heart that her own experience would parallel that of Jacob, who met God at the least likely

87

time and place, but who was a new man from that day on. The rhythm of the stanzas stayed with her as she meditated and prayed. Then, without too much conscious effort, she began to write down some lines of her own in the same metrical pattern that Sarah Adams had used in writing her poetic version of Jacob at Bethel. Her poem began:

More love to Thee, O Christ, More love to Thee;
Hear Thou the prayer I make, On bended knee.
This is my earnest plea, More love O Christ, to Thee; More love
    to Thee.

She completed four stanzas that same evening, but did not show them to her husband until thirteen years later. The hymn was first printed in leaflet form in 1869, and in a hymnal the next year, 1870.

Although she wrote five books before her death in 1878, in her sixtieth year, one of them, "Stepping Heavenward" becoming a best-seller, she lives on in the hearts of Christian people because of her New Testament version of Sarah Flower Adams' Old Testament hymn.

30.

MY FAITH LOOKS UP TO THEE

Unlike Tennyson, whose best poem was his last, "Crossing the Bar" being written during the poet's eighty-first year, Ray Palmer's best was his first, written when he was only twenty-two. In the fall of 1830, the young Yale graduate went to New York City as a teacher in a select school for young ladies, directed by a lady who was connected with St. George's Church.

There, he divided his time between teaching and studying theology, residing with the family of the director of the school. Accustomed from childhood to the expression of what his heart felt in the form of verse, he sat at his desk one night in the early winter of 1830, and began writing another poem. It was an hour "when Christ in the riches of His grace and love was so vividly apprehended as to fill the soul with the deepest emotion." With no thought of writing a hymn and without the slightest intention of penning a poem that any other eyes should ever read, he wrote six stanzas in the unusual 6.6.4.6.6.6.4. meter, the first of which read:

My faith looks up to Thee, Thou Lamb of Calvary, Saviour
    Divine;
Now hear me while I pray; Take all my guilt away;
O let me from this day, Be wholly Thine.

He was so deeply stirred that he stained the closing lines with abundant tears. Before he retired he wrote these words in his diary, "I wrote tonight a simple poem. I wrote just what I felt with little effort. I recollect that I penned the last words with tender emotion."

Later he copied the stanzas in a small morocco-covered book which he always carried with him for just such purposes, and promptly forgot all about them.

89

In the fall of 1832, two years after he had written what was to become his most famous hymn, Ray Palmer was visiting in Boston when he chanced to meet his friend, Dr. Lowell Mason, on a busy street. Mason, the father of American hymnology, asked the young man if he had come across any good new hymns for a "Hymn and Tune Book" which he planned to publish shortly with the assistance of Dr. Hastings of New York. Palmer hesitantly referred to his little book, so reluctant was he to let anyone else read the lines in which he had recorded his profound and moving spiritual experience. But when Mason read the stanzas, he asked for a copy. The men stepped into a store together and a copy was made which Mason put in his pocket. Upon arriving home, the musician read over the verses carefully, and was so much impressed that he composed an original tune for them which he named "Olivet."

Two days later the two men met again on another busy Boston street. Scarcely waiting to greet the young poet, Dr. Mason exclaimed, "Mr. Palmer, you may live many years and do many good things, but I think you will be best known to posterity as the author of 'My Faith Looks Up to Thee.'"

The poet was ordained as a Congregational minister in 1835, holding pastorates and executive positions in Maine and New York. When he and his wife celebrated their golden wedding anniversary in 1882, a friend paid him this tribute, "The grandest privilege which God has ever given to His children upon earth and which He gives to comparatively few is to write a noble Christian hymn to be accepted by the churches, to be sung by reverent and loving hearts in different lands and in different tongues, and which still shall be sung as the future opens its brightening centuries."

Although he wrote other hymns and translated from the Latin such poetic gems as "Come Holy Ghost in Love" and "Jesus, Thou Joy of Loving Hearts" before his death in 1887, English-speaking Christians are unanimous in agreeing that Ray Palmer's first hymn was his best.

31.

NEARER MY GOD TO THEE

About a hundred years after it was printed, an American business man, David Randall, sold a copy of "Hymns and Anthems" (London, 1841) for $25.00. The century-old book brought that amount because it contained the first printing of the hymn "Nearer My God to Thee" by Sarah Flower Adams.

When editor Benjamin Flower, her father, was imprisoned in Newgate Prison for criticizing the political activities of the Bishop of Landlaff, in the columns of his paper, "The Cambridge Intelligencer," one of his visitors was Eliza Gould, a Devonshire school teacher, who admired his writings and views. Friendship ripened into love and upon his release from jail she became his second wife, and the stepmother of two talented girls, Sarah and Elizabeth Flower.

Later, Sarah was to meet her future husband in circumstances almost as unusual. She contributed to a journal, "The Repository," edited by Unitarian minister, Rev. William J. Fox. Her articles appeared in issues which also carried literary contributions from an inventive engineer, William B. Adams. In 1834, when she was thirty-one, they were married. Gifted as an actress, she starred as "Lady Macbeth" in a London theatre in 1837, but gave up what promised to be a brilliant stage career when she found her strength unequal to the task. She is described as "tall and singularly beautiful, with noble and regular features, in manner gay and impulsive, her conversation witty and sparkling."

Rev. Mr. Fox, pastor of the Unitarian Church known as the South Place Religious Society, Finsbury, called on the two gifted sisters one afternoon in 1840. "I am compiling this new hymnal," he explained, "because none of the hymnbooks that are available seem to meet the needs of our particular congregation.

And I am quite anxious to get the materials to the printer as soon as possible."

"So you want us to finish our verses and music within the next few weeks," Sarah Flower Adams said.

"Yes, if you can possibly do so, Mrs. Adams," the minister answered. "How are you getting along with the new tunes?"

"I've corrected and edited about half of the one hundred fifty tunes, Mr. Fox," Elizabeth replied. "And I want to write a few more tunes myself for some of Sarah's poems before I return the manuscripts."

"Excellent," said the pastor. "Our people will be more interested in the new hymnal when they know so many of the stanzas and so much of the music came from two of our most gifted communicants."

The discussion turned to the sermon the minister was planning for the coming Sunday. Picking up a Bible, he told them he wanted to preach about the story of Jacob at Bethel, from Genesis 28:10-22.

"Is there a hymn about Jacob's dream with which to conclude the service?" Sarah asked.

"None that I know of," he replied.

Eliza interrupted, "There's a new idea, Sarah. Why not write your own hymn about Jacob's dream for the new hymnal?"

"Splendid," Mr. Fox added.

Later that day, Sarah Adams read the story of Jacob over several times, absorbing the atmosphere and feeling the dramatic movement of the Old Testament narrative. Then, picking up her pen, she wrote the complete story in five stanzas, which began:

Nearer, my God, to Thee; Nearer to Thee; E'en though it be a cross That raiseth me.
Still all my song shall be, Nearer, my God, to thee; Nearer to Thee.

The new hymn was sung for the first time in South Place Chapel, London, in the fall of 1840, and was included in the 1841 (second) edition of Fox's "Hymns and Anthems." For the two editions of this book, Sarah contributed sixty-three hymns and Elizabeth one-hundred-fifty tunes.

Because the author was attending a Unitarian Church when she wrote the hymn, and because it contains no reference to Jesus, the hymn was rather severely criticized for a while. However, on the wings of Lowell Mason's tune, composed in 1856, it has won its way into the hearts of believers all over the world.

When it was sung as his favorite hymn at the funeral of President William McKinley in 1901 and by the hundreds who went down with the Titanic in 1912, its place in Christian hymnody was assured.

Elizabeth Flower died of tuberculosis in 1847; her sister, Sarah, contracting it from her while acting as her nurse, passed away twenty months later, August 11, 1848.

32.

O JESUS THOU ART STANDING

The author of this hymn, Bishop William Walsham How (1823-1897) practiced what he preached. He often said, "A good hymn should be like a good prayer—simple, real, earnest and reverent." His best hymns are just that.

English-born How was an unusual man in that he declined the Bishopric of the great city of Manchester without even telling his wife it had been offered him; and on another occasion he refused the Bishopric of Durham, England, which carried with it an enviable prestige as well as a large income. Later he accepted the position of Suffragan Bishop of London, his area including the worst slums of East London, carrying with it a small salary and no social prestige. Nicknamed the "Omnibus Bishop," because, unlike some high ecclesiastics who wore fancy vestments and rode in private coaches, he rode the buses with his people, he was only concerned with how much he could make his life count for the Lord.

Following his graduation from Oxford with a Master's Degree in 1847, he entered the ministry of the Church of England. After serving two appointments, he became rector of Whittington, Shropshire, in 1851, remaining there for twenty-eight years. It was for this congregation, during the years 1858-1871, that he wrote most of his hymns.

A painting and a poem gave him the inspiration for "O Jesus Thou Art Standing." The painting was a copy of Holman Hunt's famous work, "The Light of the World." The original was finished in 1854 and hung in Keble College. Within two years it had all of England talking. Widespread disapproval greeted it at first, but when John Ruskin came to the painter's defense with his graphic interpretation of the picture, opposing voices soon died down. The picture was gradually accepted and copies made available for those who were able to purchase them.

One evening in the early spring of 1867, How's forty-fourth year, he was studying a copy of this painting in the light of Ruskin's interpretation. He read what the literary genius had written. "On the left-hand side of the picture is seen this door of the human soul. It is fast-barred; its bars and nails are rusty; it is knitted and bound to its stanchions by creeping tendrils of ivy, showing that it has never been opened. A bat hovers about it; its threshold is overgrown with brambles, nettles and fruitless corn—the wild grass 'whereof the mower filleth not his hand nor he that bindeth the sheaves to his bosom.' Christ approaches it in the night-time. Christ, in His everlasting offices of Prophet, Priest and King. He wears the white robe, representing the power of the Spirit upon Him; the jeweled robe and breast-plate, representing the sacerdotal investiture; the rayed crown of gold, inwoven with the crown of thorns; not dead thorns, but now bearing soft leaves for the healing of the nations."

He read on about the meaning of the lighted lantern in the Lord's hand and the symbolism of the light about the Master's head, and was deeply moved by what Ruskin had written.

Sometime later he read passages from Jean Ingelow's poem, "Brothers and a Sermon" and recalled how closely the poem paralleled the painting. In it, the writer pictured a parson proclaiming the great invitation from Revelation 3:20, "Behold, I stand at the door and knock; if any man will hear my voice and open the door, I will come in to him and I will sup with him and he with me." He read aloud the last four lines of the long poem, "Speak then, O rich and strong; Open, O happy young, ere yet the hand of Him who knocks, wearied at last, forbear; The patient foot its thankless quest refrain, The wounded heart forevermore withdraw." The pathos of the verses impressed him so forcibly that he read them over several times. Finally, putting the book of poetry down, he scribbled on an old scrap of paper some ideas for a new hymn. Later he explained, "I altered them a good deal subsequently, but after the hymn left my hands it was never altered in any way." His first stanza contained these lines:

O Jesus, Thou art standing Outside the fast-closed door,
In lowly patience waiting To pass the threshold o'er;
We bear the name of Christians, His name and sign we bear;
O shame, thrice shame upon us! To keep Him standing there.

The three stanzas of this hymn were first published the year of their composition in a supplement to "Psalms and Hymns" prepared by How and Rev. Thomas Morrell. In addition to this hymn, he is known for "O Word of God Incarnate," "For All the Saints Who from Their Labors Rest," "Summer Suns Are Glowing," "We Give Thee but Thine Own." Of his sixty hymns, these are still in common usage after the passing of nearly a century.

While not claiming to be a poet in the sense in which Watts and Wesley were poets, he has sung songs that have outlived all his other literary works, and "O Jesus Thou Art Standing," will continue to remind future generations that Christ will enter only if we open the door of the human heart before which He stands.

33.

O LITTLE TOWN OF BETHLEHEM

Episcopal Bishop Phillips Brooks was such a remarkable man that when he died, a five-year-old girl said to her mother, "Oh, mama, how happy the angels will be." Only a radiantly angelic character could merit such a reward.

But his life was not always crowned with such honor and deserved praise. As a Latin teacher in Boston he was a miserable and conspicuous failure. It was only when he entered the Christian ministry that he found himself, and became the hero among men, the saint among sages and the prince of American preachers.

In 1865, while he was rector of Holy Trinity Church, Philadelphia, the thirty-year-old minister made a trip to the Holy Land. His congregation was so devoted to him that they were loath to give him up even for such an eventful trip, and one Church paper wrote, "He will go accompanied with the prayers of thousands for his happy journeying and his safe return."

On December 24, Christmas Eve, he made the trip from Jerusalem to Bethlehem on horseback. He noted in his diary, "Before dark we rode out of town to the field where they say the shepherds saw the star. It is a fenced piece of ground with a cave in it, in which strangely enough, they put the shepherds." Later that night he attended religious services in an ancient basilica said to have been built by Emperor Constantine early in the fourth century. The service lasted five hours and made quite an impression upon the mind and heart of the young clergyman. He returned home with "Palestine singing in his soul," little dreaming that three years would pass before the seed planted on that trip would finally bear fruit.

As he planned his services for Christmas 1868, the pastor thought again of the Holy Land and the inspiring visit he had enjoyed there many months before. Combining preparation with memory, looking forward and backward at the same time, he was moved to express his feelings in a beautiful Christmas carol, written especially with the children of his flock in mind. The new hymn he wanted them to sing that Advent contained these lovely lines:

O little town of Bethlehem, How still we see thee lie;
Above thy deep and dreamless sleep The silent stars go by.
Yet in thy dark streets shineth The everlasting light;
The hopes and fears of all the years Are met in thee tonight.

The following day, when Lewis Redner, Church organist as well as Sunday School Superintendent, came into the pastor's study, Brooks handed him a sheet of paper on which he had written the five stanzas of his new hymn.

"Lewis," he said, "why not write a new tune for my hymn? If it turns out to be a good tune, I'll name it 'St. Lewis' after you."

The organist looked at the stanzas and replied, "I'll do what I can, but if it is a success, why not name the tune 'St. Phillip' after you?"

Although he had ample time in which to compose the new tune, Redner delayed writing anything down until it was almost too late. "No inspiration," he complained. The night before the minister planned for the children to sing his new song, Redner had not come up with any music whatsoever. On Christmas Eve, at the very last minute, the inspiration came. He fell asleep worrying about the music, and woke up suddenly in the middle of the night with a new tune ringing in his ears. He wrote down the melody as quickly as he could on a piece of paper close by, and went back to sleep. Early the next morning he harmonized the melody and the children sang it for the first time on December 27, 1868.

Brooks later paid tribute to his organist-friend without embarrassing him by naming the tune after him, but with a different spelling of the name, calling it "St. Louis." The music has thus no connection whatsoever with the city of the same name, though some have tried in vain to establish one.

While Brooks (1835-1893) and Redner (1831-1908) remained bachelors all their lives, they lived to see the Christmas carol in which they collaborated become one of the favorites of children the world over.

34.

O LOVE THAT WILT NOT LET ME GO

When doctors told fifteen-year-old George Matheson that his shadowy eyesight would soon become total blindness, he ignored their diagnosis and went ahead with his plans. Enrolling in the University of Glasgow, Scotland, in 1857, he graduated in 1861, a youth of nineteen. The fact that the great John Milton, author of "Paradise Lost" and "Paradise Regained," had written a famous sonnet "On His Blindness" was little consolation to the young graduate, who refused to be numbered among his fellow sufferers who "also serve who only stand and wait." He lost his eyesight during the years he was studying theology in preparation for the Christian ministry. His devoted sisters rallied to his side, mastering Hebrew, Greek and Latin in order to be his faithful assistants. But even their love and devotion could not mend the heart which broke when his fiancee broke their engagement, returned his ring, and wrote something to the effect that "I cannot see my way clear to go through life bound by the chains of marriage to a blind man."

George Matheson never married, but he did become one of the most poetic and eloquent preachers of his day. As parish minister at Innellan, Argylshire, a popular seaside resort in western Scotland not far from the mouth of the River Clyde, he was deeply beloved throughout his whole parish. It was there, in 1882, his fortieth year, that one of his sisters married. For the popular blind pastor, her wedding brought back memories of heart-break and personal tragedy. From the depths of his despair, he reached out in faith and laid hold of the unchanging love of God, a love that "wilt not let me go," and penned the four stanzas of his greatest hymn:

O love that wilt not let me go, I rest my weary soul in thee;
I give thee back the life I owe, That in thine ocean depths its
  flow
May richer, fuller be.

Four years later he accepted the pulpit of the two-thousand member St. Bernard's Church, Edinburgh, where he reached the zenith of his power and influence. Before his death in 1906 he wrote some of the best inspirational literature in the English language, as well as another well-known hymn, "Make Me a Captive, Lord, and Then I Shall Be Free."

The secret of his successful and useful life is found in the stanzas of his best-known hymn, wherein he yields himself to the "Light that followest all my way" and tastes the "Joy that seekest me through pain." Before the "Cross that lifteth up my head," he says, "I lay in dust life's glory dead, And from the ground there blossoms red Life that shall endless be."

35.

ONWARD, CHRISTIAN SOLDIERS

Rev. Sabine Baring-Gould was not content merely to propose to his future bride; he actually performed his own marriage ceremony. It must have been quite an experience to hear the officiating minister ask himself, "Will you, Sabine, take this woman, Grace, to be your lawful wedded wife?," and then reply to himself, "I will." Anyway, when the bride kissed the groom she was kissing the minister at the same time. Whether he took the fee out of his left pocket and deposited it in his right after the ceremony has never been determined.

He was ordained as a clergyman of the Church of England in 1864, after taking his Bachelor's and Master's degrees from Clare College, Cambridge, England. While serving as curate of St. John's Church, Horbury Bridge, Yorkshire, he planned a special sermon on "Missions" one Sunday night. Failing to find an appropriate hymn with which to conclude the service, he wrote one of his own, entitled "An Evening Hymn for Missions." The first stanza contained these beautiful lines:

> Now the day is over, Night is drawing nigh;
> Shadows of the evening Steal across the sky.

Remembering a simple melody he had heard during a bicycle trip through Germany several summers before, he harmonized it as his own tune for these new stanzas, giving the tune the name "Eudoxia."

Meanwhile, he was writing books on a wide variety of subjects, from the lives of the Saints to his experiences with ghosts in old English castles. Pentecost, the Sunday that comes fifty days after Easter, is known in England as Whitsunday, an abbreviation of White-Sunday, from the custom of wearing white on that occasion. The day following, Whitmonday, is a legal as

101

well as a Church holiday. On Whitmonday, 1865, Baring-Gould arranged an outing for the children of his parish, including a hike from his own Church to a nearby village. Knowing that children like to march, and also how difficult it is for their elders to keep them together unless they are marching, he asked his helpers to find "a good marching hymn" to help them keep order during the proposed hike. When they could find no appropriate hymn, several of his parishioners suggested that, as he had written his own Missionary Hymn, he proceed to write his own Marching Hymn.

Unpertubed, the brilliant thirty-one-year-old pastor did just that, writing the new stanzas in the same metrical pattern in which he had composed his earlier ones, 6.5.6.5.D. (The first and third lines having six syllables; the second and fourth containing five syllables, with the whole pattern being doubled, into a poem of eight lines.) With no thought of writing a hymn for a nation at war, little dreaming that his stanzas would ever be so misconstrued, and taking a theme from Haydn's "Symphony in D" for his music, he dashed off five stanzas which began with these thrilling lines:

> Onward Christian Soldiers, Marching as to war,
> With the cross of Jesus Going on before;
> Christ the royal Master Leads against the foe;
> Forward into battle, See His banners go.

Although he lived to the age of ninety and wrote over eighty-five books before his death in 1924, Baring-Gould is remembered as the author of one of the loveliest evening hymns and the most militant marching hymn in all Christendom.

36.

PEACE PERFECT PEACE

One of Fanny Crosby's favorite poems was: "I think that life is not too long and therefore I determine, That many people read a song who will not read a sermon." Be that as it may, one is hard put to decide whether John Wesley's sermons were the inspiration of brother Charles' hymns or whether it worked the other way around.

But we know without a doubt that it was a sermon preached one Sunday morning in August 1875 by Canon Gibbon, the Vicar of Harrogate, England, that inspired a visiting minister to write "Peace Perfect Peace." The visitor was Rev. Edward H. Bickersteth, vicar of Christ Church, Hampstead, who was spending the summer holidays at Harrogate. Canon Gibbon preached from Isaiah 26:3, "Thou wilt keep him in perfect peace whose mind is stayed on thee," and his message had a profound effect on the fifty-year-old visitor. That very Sunday afternoon, Bickersteth visited an aged, dying relative, Archdeacon Hill, of Liverpool, and found him troubled and concerned about his impending death. To comfort him, the minister quoted the text of the morning sermon, and spoke of the strength he had received from the message.

"What did he say about this perfect peace?" the older man asked.

"He explained that in the original Hebrew the verse read 'Thou wilt keep him in peace peace, whose mind is stayed on thee.' "

"Peace, peace?" the dying man asked.

"Yes. He told us that in repetition the Hebrew writer conveyed the idea of perfection. The translators of the Authorized Version of 1611 knew that the Hebrews wrote in this idiom, so, instead of repeating the word 'peace' twice, they translated it so all could understand what was in the author's mind; hence 'perfect peace.' "

To further bolster the faith of his friend, the visitor quoted verses from the Ninetieth Psalm and repeated some of the stanzas he had written on them, which began:

O God, the Rock of Ages, Who evermore hast been
What time the tempest rages, Our dwelling-place serene.

Later the conversation drifted back to the morning sermon. The older man kept repeating the verse from which the minister had preached, grasping at the words in a desperate effort to strengthen his own faith in the face of death.

"What else did Canon Gibbon say about this perfect peace?" he asked.

"He showed us the difference between tranquillity, the absence of storm and strife, and peace, the ability to weather the storm and strife, this Christian peace being an active possession, not a passive mood; a conviction of the mind as well as a condition of the soul."

Picking up his prayer book, the minister read the Collect for Peace: "O God, from whom all holy desires, all good counsels, and all just works do proceed, give unto thy servants that peace which the world cannot give; that our hearts may be set to obey thy commandments, and also that by thee, we, being defended from the fear of our enemies, may pass our time in rest and quietness, through the merits of Jesus Christ, our Saviour, Amen."

Throughout the conversation, Dr. Bickersteth felt the urge to write, so, when his friend dropped off to sleep, he took up a sheet of paper and then and there began to write down several stanzas. Taking the idea of "peace peace" meaning "perfect peace" he combined the teachings of both and formed the phrase "peace, perfect peace." The first line of each stanza asked a question, implying that there were too many obstacles to the attainment of such peace. The second line of each stanza answered the questions with an affirmation of faith that could not be denied. When Mr. Hill woke, the author read the stanzas to him, and rejoiced when they brought comfort to his troubled heart.

When he returned home later that afternoon, as the family gathered for their customary tea, the father said, "Children, I have written a hymn," and he read his new stanzas in their hearing, beginning with these beautiful lines:

> Peace, perfect peace, in this dark world of sin?
> The blood of Jesus whispers peace within.
> Peace, perfect peace, by thronging duties pressed?
> To do the will of Jesus—this is rest.

Little did he dream that his verses would comfort his own heart, but they did, when he was the chief mourner at the grave of one of his preacher sons, Bishop Edward Bickersteth of South Tokyo, who was buried at Chiselden in 1897.

After serving with distinction as Bishop of Exeter, and publishing more than twelve volumes of prose and poetry, he died in London in 1906 in full possession of the "peace, perfect peace" about which he had sung so eloquently thirty-one years before.

37.

RESCUE THE PERISHING

Few places in the world are more depressing than New York City's Bowery and Chicago's Skid Row. While few poets would visit either one, seeking inspiration, the Bowery served as a background against which Fanny Crosby wrote one of her finest hymns, "Rescue the Perishing."

My maternal grandfather, Rev. Albert G. Ruliffson, founded the famous Bowery Mission in November, 1879. He served as President of its Board of Trustees and was active in its work until September, 1895, passing away two years later, in May, 1897. In the vestibule of the present building, around the corner from the original structure, there is a plaque to his memory bearing, in addition to some of the facts related above, the verse of Scripture which characterized his life, "If any man serve me, him will my Father honor" (John 12:26).

Fanny Crosby was sixty years old when she visited the Bowery Mission for the first time. Already famous as the author of such best-sellers as "A Blind Girl and Other Poems" (1844), "Monteresy and Other Poems" (1849) and "A Wreath of Columbia's Flowers" (1858) she had turned her talents to the writing of hymns and gospel songs. Inspired by Robert Lowry, William Bradbury, W. H. Doane, Ira D. Sankey, George F. Root and other well-known musicians and composers, she had already written such perennial favorites as "Jesus Keep Me Near the Cross" and "Draw Me Nearer."

When she attended the Mission one night in 1880, she little dreamed that it would provide the inspiration for one of her most popular religious poems. When asked to speak at the close of the service, she rose and said, "There may be a man here who has gone as far as a man can go. If he is present, I want to shake hands with him." A man *did* come forward at the close of the

106

meeting and shook her hand. But when she invited him to become a Christian, he muttered "What's the difference? Nobody cares for me." The poet assured him that Jesus cared for him as He cared for all people everywhere. With that he promised to be present the very next night and accept Christ as his Lord and Saviour if she would be there too. The next evening he made his peace with God in her presence. Following that initial visit, Fanny Crosby went often to the Bowery Mission. Her words of encouragement brought many lost souls back into the joy of the Kingdom of God. On another evening that very same year she gave this invitation, "If there is a lad here who has wandered from his mother's Christian teachings, I would like to pray with him at the altar at the close of the service." A young man came forward and they prayed together. He rose from his knees with a new light in his eyes, and said, "Now I can meet my mother in heaven for I have found her God." Later a friend remarked, "Isn't it wonderful what these rescue missions are doing?" She could hardly wait to get home to her desk and begin writing,

> Rescue the perishing, Care for the dying,
> Snatch them in pity from sin and the grave;
> Weep o'er the erring one, Lift up the fallen;
> Tell them of Jesus, The mighty to save.

Set to music by W. H. Doane, wealthy Cincinnati business man and composer, it became one of the few hymns the author considered "outstanding."

Twenty-three years later, when the poet was speaking in the Y.M.C.A. in Lynn, Massachusetts, she told the story of "Rescue the Perishing." Several men came up to greet her when she finished her talk, one of them asking, "Do you remember me?" She shook her head, so he said, "I was the young man who found God that night in the Bowery Mission. Since then I have tried to live a consistent Christian life. And my song is no longer 'Rescue the Perishing.' It is another one you wrote which begins, 'Saviour, more than life to me, I am clinging, clinging, close to Thee.'"

Although she wrote hymns and songs by the thousands and lived to see her books sold by the millions before her death at the age of ninety-five, her life, characterized by unfailing joy, unflagging zeal and unwavering faith, lives on in the poems now dear to the hearts of all Christendom. This vital Christian faith is seen no clearer than in a comment she once made about Tennyson's great poem, "Crossing the Bar." "If I were writing that poem," she said, "I would change one word in the last stanza. Instead of saying, 'I *hope* to see my Pilot face to face,' I would write, 'I *know* I'll see my Pilot face to face, When I have crossed the bar.' "

38.

ROCK OF AGES

Some ministers regard playing cards as passports to hell. But if conservative Calvinist, Augustus Montague Toplady, had not had the six-of-diamonds in his pocket one memorable afternoon in 1775, Christendom might have missed one of its most heavenly hymns.

English-born, and Irish-educated, Toplady became an Anglican clergyman in 1762. Some years later, when serving as minister of a Church of French Calvinists in Leicester Fields, London, he penned his immortal stanzas on the only piece of paper he could find, the above-mentioned playing card, while taking shelter in a great cleft rock in Burrington Gorge, Somersetshire, England. Two standard British encyclopedias attest to this fact, strange as it seems!

But Toplady was not one to go around hiding in rocky clefts all the time. He "fought the good fight of faith" with words, as deftly and skillfully as an insulted French nobleman fought with swords. A strict and devout follower of John Calvin, he believed that God saved only "the elect," of which, naturally, he was one! John Wesley, on the other hand, preached with equal fervor and as much Scriptural authority, that God's free grace was available to all. "Whosoever will may come," he proclaimed. Toplady refused to recognize the validity of Wesley's argument, and proceeded to tear it to pieces in the columns of "The Gospel Magazine" which he edited.

"Wesley is guilty of Satanic shamelessness," he wrote. He "acts the part of a lurking, sly assassin" while "uniting the sophistry of a Jesuit with the authority of a pope."

Wesley answered "the vain boaster" with these words, "I do not fight with chimney-sweeps."

Angered by that remark, the editor, in the March, 1776 issue

109

of his journal, compared the "debt of sin" with England's "national debt." "At the rate of one sin each second," he wrote, "every man at twenty is guilty of 630,720,000 sins; at fifty, of 1,576,800,000; and at eighty of 2,522,880,000." Since no one can pay off such a debt, we rely on Christ alone to redeem us, he concluded. Then followed the caption: "A living and dying prayer for the holiest believer in the world" and three six-line stanzas which began:

Rock of ages, cleft for me, Let me hide myself in thee;
Let the water and the blood, From thy riven side which flowed,
Be of sin the double cure, Cleanse from wrath and make me
    pure.

The author lived only two years after his hymn was published, dying of tuberculosis in 1778, at thirty-eight, with these words on his lips, "My prayers are all converted into praise." His complete "Works" were published in six volumes sixteen years after his death.

Although he and the Wesleys were theological opponents, each accusing the other of misunderstanding the Gospel, they were much closer than they realized. Charles Wesley had anticipated his critic by thirty years. In his book, "Hymns on the Lord's Supper," published when Toplady was just a young boy, Wesley had included as, Number twenty-seven, a new hymn, beginning with this line:

Rock of Israel, cleft for me.

So, instead of singing a solo, Toplady was actually singing a duet with his bitterest rival and severest critic. Maybe when he knocked at the gates of Heaven, St. Peter told him he would have to recite the stanzas of Wesley's "Jesus, Lover of My Soul" before he could get in. And, no doubt, he told Charles Wesley he could not enter unless he could recite the three stanzas of Toplady's hymn, "Rock of Ages."

While neither man had a place in his heart for the other, the heart of the Almighty was big enough to include them both!

39.

SAFE IN THE ARMS OF JESUS

Many of Fanny Crosby's popular hymns and gospel songs were written backwards. Instead of writing a poem for someone else to set to music, she wrote quite a few of her stanzas to fit somebody else's tunes.

Born in a little cottage in Southeast, Putnam County, New York, March 24, 1820, she was permanently blinded when six weeks old because of the ignorance of a country doctor who applied hot poultices to her inflamed eyes. Before she was a year old, her father, John Crosby, died. Her mother and grandmother supervised the girl's training during her early years. When she was nine, the family moved to Ridgefield, Connecticut where they spent six "beautiful and beneficial years." During her ninth year she wrote her first poem. Going out into the fields one afternoon she asked God to use her for some good, pure and noble purpose; there she dedicated her young life to Him. When she came home a few hours later, she jotted down her first poem. Considering the poet's age and physical condition, the lines are among the most beautiful in all literature.

Oh what a happy soul am I, Although I cannot see;
I am resolved that in this world Contented I will be.
How many blessings I enjoy That other people don't;
To weep and sigh because I'm blind, I cannot and I won't.

Little wonder that God worked miracles through her. Before her death in 1915 at the age of ninety-five, she had written more hymns, songs and poems than anyone else since the beginning of the Christian era. In 1858, she and Alexander Van Alstyne, a blind musician and instructor in the New York City Institution for the Blind, were married, but she continued to write and publish her works under her well-known maiden name. She and her husband united with the Thirtieth Street Methodist Church in New York.

One afternoon during the summer of 1868, a prominent businessman and Christian layman, William H. Doane, who composed music as a hobby, knocked at Fanny Crosby's door. When he was admitted, he rushed up to the blind poet and said, "Miss Fanny, I have exactly forty minutes before my train leaves for Cincinnati, and I must take that train." When she asked the reason for his call in view of that fact, he explained, "There is to be a great state-wide Sunday School convention in Cincinnati next month. In addition to the large delegations of adults, many young people and children are expected to be present. I want a new hymn which I can introduce for the first time at this convention, to capture the hearts and imaginations of the young people and children." Fanny Crosby smiled, looked up at him with her sightless eyes, and said, "You have already composed the tune, haven't you?" "How did you know?" Mr. Doane replied. "Woman's intuition," she answered, graciously. "Since you know, you might as well listen to it," he added. "And listen closely, because my train leaves in thirty-five minutes and I want to take that new hymn with me when I go."

Turning to the piano he sat down and played his new tune in a rousing and stirring manner. When he finished, Fanny Crosby said, "There is a Bible verse that has been ringing in my mind and heart all day. 'Underneath are the everlasting arms.' " "What about the hymn?" asked Mr. Doane anxiously. "It's right there, William," his hostess explained; "right there in that verse. Your music says 'Safe in the arms of Jesus.' What could be more appropriate for boys and girls at a Sunday School convention?" Mr. Doane consulted his watch. "Just thirty minutes left," he said, somewhat impatiently. She replied, "You will have your hymn." Going to her desk, she took out a piece of paper, found her pen, sat down and began to write. After putting down several lines, she asked Mr. Doane to play his tune over a few times while she prepared her stanzas. As he played, she continued to write. When she was through, she folded the sheet of paper, placed it in an envelope and handed it to her friend. "Here it is, William. You can read it on the train. Now, hurry. You don't want to be late." He thanked her, said his

"Goodbyes," grabbed his hat and rushed for the carriage that was awaiting him in front of the house. Enroute to Cincinnati on the train, he opened the envelope, took out the piece of paper and read what she had written to fit his music. The first stanza and chorus were as follows:

> Safe in the arms of Jesus, Safe on His gentle breast:
> There by His love o'ershaded, Sweetly my soul shall rest.
> Hark! Tis the voice of angels, Borne on a song to me—
> Over the fields of glory, Over the jasper sea.

> (Repeat the first two lines for the Chorus.)

Although she wrote between seven and eight thousand poems during her lifetime, at the time of her death few equaled in popularity the words she wrote to fit a tune composed by an Ohio businessman for a Sunday School convention.

40.

SAVED BY GRACE

While Fanny Crosby did not write her first hymn until she was forty-four, she made up for lost time and turned out over five-thousand more before her death at ninety-five.

Her first, written February 5, 1864, began with these lines: "We are going, we are going, To a home beyond the skies, Where the fields are robed in beauty And the sunlight never dies." Then followed a flood of hymns and songs, produced at the rate of over three a week for more than fifty years.

The first of her compositions to be widely received and used was written in 1868. The title was suggested by her friend, Mr. W. H. Doane, Cincinnati businessman and composer. "He asked me to write a hymn on 'Pass me not O gentle Saviour,'" said the author. "I worked on it until I felt it was a real prayer from the heart. The first verse was my soul pleading for the Saviour to hear my cry; then I found a throne of mercy and the spring of all my comfort, and my soul rested not, but continued to cry, 'Saviour, Saviour, hear my humble cry,' in the words of the refrain." Some see a similarity between Mr. Doane's tune and the music of the Hawaiian national song, "Aloha." He composed his tune for her stanzas in 1868 and Queen Liliuokalani did not copyright her song until 1884, sixteen years later. However, in Fritz Kreisler's biography, the famous violinist speaks of "Aloha" as a "Viennese ditty," entitled "We'll Go to Nussdorf Right Away" (Nussdorf is a suburb of Vienna). He says that it was offered to the Queen by a German-born violin teacher from San Francisco who was commissioned by Her majesty to write the national anthem. Later she knighted him for composing Hawaii's most popular song. An article in the August 22, 1953 issue of "The Saturday Evening Post" states that "Aloha" is an old hymn tune, "Rock by the Sea," with new words. A history of Christian work in the islands, published by Park Street Church, Boston, which sent out the first missionaries, mentions the singing of great hymns on the part of recent converts, and their enthusiasm for English and American hymns and songs long before Fanny Crosby published her first hymn. Consequently, the similarity must be purely coincidental.

When her husband died, she wrote these moving lines after finding a withered leaf among his souvenirs, " 'Tis only a leaf, a withered leaf, But its story is fraught with pain; 'Twas the gift of one who is far away And will never return again. He will never return, But I know ere long My spirit with his will be; And the old time love shall be sweeter there, Where I know he waits for me." Shortly before her death in 1915 she wrote her last published hymn which began with these words, "At evening time it shall be light." Just before her death she penned her last lines, "You will reach the river brink, Some sweet day, bye and bye."

In 1891 she attended a mid-week Prayer Meeting service at which Dr. Howard Crosby spoke. He talked on the Twenty-third Psalm, using "Grace" as his subject. When he died very suddenly that very same week, blind Fanny Crosby said to herself, "I wonder what my first impression of heaven will be." A moment later she suddenly answered her own question, "Why, my eyes will be opened and I will see my Saviour face to face." When her publisher-friend, Mr. L. H. Bigelow, asked her to write a hymn on "Grace" a few days later, she wrote the four stanzas and chorus of "Saved by Grace" in less than an hour.

In 1894 while she was visiting friends at Northfield, Massachusetts, she was invited to address one of the religious conferences there by Ira D. Sankey, famous song-leader and composer. After talking for a few minutes, she concluded her remarks by reciting the poem she had written three years before on "Grace." A reporter from a London newspaper took her hymn with him to England where it was published in a newspaper. When Sankey found the stanzas in print he prevailed upon George Stebbins to compose the music.

When Fanny Crosby died in 1915, her prayer was answered, because she had prayed in the chorus of her famous song, "And I shall see Him face to face, And tell the story—saved by grace."

41.

SHALL WE GATHER AT THE RIVER

Even though Rev. Robert Lowry often said, "I would rather preach a gospel sermon than write a hymn," he lives on in his hymns rather than in his sermons. In fact, were it not for his hymns and gospel songs, his name would hardly be remembered at all, although he did not take up the serious study of music until after his fortieth birthday.

While it may seem unusual to expect a college professor to produce a "Hit Parade" song, Mr. Lowry, one-time professor of rhetoric at his Alma Mater, Bucknell University, wrote the words and music of the most popular "tear jerker" of his day. Originally entitled "The Absent Child," the song is more familiarly known by its first line, "Where is my wandering boy tonight?" Doubtless this song was suggested by just such a question addressed to him by one of his parishioners as he made his regular pastoral visits from house to house.

When asked how he did it, the popular Baptist clergyman replied, "I watch my moods, and when anything strikes me, whether words or music, no matter where I am, at home, or on the street, I jot it down. Often the margin of a newspaper or the back of an envelope serves as a notebook. Frequently the words and music have been written at the same time."

Lowry made a distinct contribution to Sunday School music when he made good use of the "Chorus" or "Refrain." He felt it was needed, not only to complete the meaning of the stanzas but also to enable the small children who could not read to sing with the adults who could. Consequently, he taught the "Refrain" to the children and encouraged them to sing it with the elders after every stanza.

Following pastorates in Baptist Churches in West Chester, Pennsylvania, and New York City, he moved to Brooklyn, New

York to become the minister of a Baptist congregation there. The summer of 1864 was unusually hot and humid. While life in a city is bad enough during days of intense heat, the people were further burdened when an epidemic began sweeping through the streets and alleys of the crowded metropolis. Person after person was laid low and the epidemic, instead of subsiding, seemed to rage with increased fury with each passing day. Hundreds were dead and hundreds more lay dying. Robert Lowry faithfully visited from house to house, comforting the sick and giving solace to the bereaved. Over and over his people would ask, "Pastor, we have parted at the river of death. Will we meet again at the river of life?" He would assure them that their family circles, now broken, would be complete again "at the river of life that flows by the throne of God," taking the figure of speech from Revelation 22:1, "And he showed me a pure river of water of life, clear as crystal, proceeding out of the throne of God and of the Lamb." He repeated this promise to hundreds of families as home after home was draped in mourning and as friends and acquaintances were dying in large numbers.

Late one afternoon, when the weary pastor came into his living room, with the heat more oppressive than usual and the number of the dying more numerous, he seated himself at his little organ to try to find relief and release in music, and to give vent to the pent-up emotions of his heart. He thought of the little children, "God's precious angels," who had succumbed to the ravages of the epidemic and of the adults who had gone on before. Suddenly the words and music of a new song began to flow out, as if by inspiration. Soon he was singing:

Shall we gather at the river, Where bright angel-feet have trod, With its crystal tide forever Flowing by the throne of God?

Answering his own question with an affirmation of Christian faith, he composed the "Chorus":

Yes, we'll gather at the river, The beautiful, the beautiful river; Gather with the saints at the river, That flows by the throne of God.

The following year, 1865, this song was published in "Happy Voices," under the title, "Mutual Recognition in the Hereafter." From there it spread to the hymnals and songbooks of many denominations.

When William Bradbury died, Dr. Lowry was selected as his successor by the Bigelow and Main Company, and in that capacity he edited many of their Sunday School songbooks. One volume, "Pure Gold," sold more than a million copies.

While "Shall We Gather at the River" has been misappropriated by some immersionist sects, abused and falsely criticized by other Church groups, and been the butt of too many a crude jest by some public speakers, it can still comfort the heart-broken and strengthen the sorrowing with the assurance of the eventual reunion with loved ones whom "we have loved long since and lost awhile."

42.

SILENT NIGHT

If the Church organ had not broken down and if the organist had not been able to strum a few chords on a guitar in an emergency, the loveliest Christmas carol of them all might never have been written.

Twenty-six-year-old Father Joseph Mohr, assistant priest at the newly erected Church of St. Nicholas in Oberndorf, in the Austrian Alps, was far from happy when his organist friend, Franz Gruber, told him that the pipe organ could not be used for the special Christmas Eve Mass scheduled for December 24, 1818. Although he trained the choir and played the organ at Arnsdorf as well as at Oberndorf, thirty-one-year-old Gruber had neither the talent nor the time to repair broken connections, restore shattered pipes or replace worn-out bellows. While Father Mohr was not desperate, he was a bit peeved at the prospects of a Midnight Mass without the traditional organ music.

To relieve his tension, he bundled himself up in his warmest winter clothes and went visiting among his humble people. Shortly after arriving at the home of one of his faithful families, a new baby was born to the poor laborer and his wife. The pastor compared that event with the birth of the Christ Child centuries earlier, and, upon arriving home a few hours later, conquered his fatigue and weariness long enough to pen four simple stanzas describing the wonder and the majesty of the first Christmas. His initial stanza contained these beautiful lines:

Silent night, Holy night! All is calm, All is bright
Round yon Virgin Mother and Child, Holy Infant, so tender and
    mild;
Sleep in heavenly peace! Sleep in heavenly peace!

When Gruber burst into the room a few moments later with the news that the organ was hopelessly beyond repair, Father Mohr handed him the slip of paper on which he had written the new stanzas. While the choir-master read them, the priest picked up a guitar in an adjoining room, and handed it to him, saying, "If we can't have the organ, at least we can have a new song. Try your hand at this."

The more Gruber protested, the stronger Mohr insisted. To quiet his friend, Gruber strummed a few simple chords on the guitar, and soon was humming an original melody that seemed to express the sentiments of the poem perfectly. At midnight the new carol was sung for the first time.

It might have remained there at Oberndorf had not Karl Mauracher come from the valley of the Zillertal to repair the organ early in 1819. Mohr asked Gruber to play the new carol for the famous organ builder and repairman, when the job was finally completed, and Mauracher fell in love with it right away. About ten years later he felt that the four gifted Strasser children, Caroline, Joseph, Andreas and Amalie, were just the ones to give the new song to the world. They renamed the carol "The Song from Heaven" and sang it wherever they went.

On Christmas Eve, 1832, they were invited to introduce it in the Royal Saxon Court Chapel in Pleissenburg Castle for the King and Queen of Saxony. The Director General of Music, Mr. Pohlenz, had heard the children singing at one of the great fairs in Leipzig where their parents went every year to sell their famous gloves. The unusual music had created an immediate sensation, the word spreading rapidly that "the four Strasser children sing like nightingales." It was at his request that the four were invited to sing for the Royal family at this special Christmas Eve celebration. Shortly thereafter, "Silent Night" took its rightful place among the most beautiful Christmas carols of the Christian world, and the passing of time has only added to its lustre.

43.

STAND UP, STAND UP FOR JESUS

The dying words of an Episcopal clergyman inspired a Presbyterian minister to write a poem. Set to a tune orginally composed for a secular song, it has become the most militant hymn American Christendom has yet produced.

The Episcopalian was young Dudley Atkins Tyng, as bold, fearless and uncompromising a preacher as his distinguished father, the Rev. Stephen H. Tyng. Following his graduation from college and seminary, and several years as his father's assistant at The Church of the Epiphany in Philadelphia, Dudley held pastorates of his own in several eastern cities before settling down as his father's successor in the large and wealthy Philadelphia church in 1854, his twenty-ninth year.

Although success as an author as well as a preacher soon followed, Dudley Tyng was not the kind of minister who "pulled his punches." As the anti-slavery sentiment grew, he expressed his convictions about the matter from the pulpit. Consequently, before his second year was up there were loud rumblings from the more conservative members of the congregation; outspoken critics were demanding his removal!

At the suggestion of some of the younger progressive leaders, Tyng resigned from The Church of the Epiphany as of November 4, 1856. With a group of faithful followers he organized "The Church of the Covenant," securing a hall on Filbert Street as a meeting place. Meanwhile, he moved with his family to a country home, "Mansion House," in the Brookfield section of Montgomery County.

In addition to his duties as pastor of a new, growing congregation, Tyng began noonday lectures at the Y.M.C.A. As his fame grew, larger and larger crowds waited upon his sermons and addresses. His boldness only increased his popularity and effectiveness.

On Tuesday, March 30, 1858, over 5,000 men gathered in Jayne's Hall (then at 621 Chestnut Street) for a mass meeting sponsored by the Y. Tyng preached from Exodus 10:11, "Ye that are men, go and serve the Lord." Over 1,000 of the men were converted; the sermon was called "one of the most successful of the times"; the entire city was being aroused; a religious awakening was gaining force.

During the sermon the preacher said, "I must tell my Master's errand, and I would rather that this right arm were amputated at the trunk than that I should come short of my duty to you in delivering God's message."

The next week he returned to his family in the country. On Tuesday, April 13, 1858, he was witnessing the operation of a corn-thrasher in his barn. Raising his arm to place his hand on the head of a mule which was walking up the inclined plane of the machine, the loose sleeve of his morning gown was caught between the cogs; the arm was lacerated severely, the main artery severed and the median nerve injured. Four days later, mortification having set in, his right arm was amputated very close to the shoulder. Anxiety prevailed for his life. Two days later, the shock to his system proved fatal.

The newspapers gave a detailed account of his passing, including his request to his faithful wife that she use her influence to bring their boys up in the ministry. The reporter wrote, "Taking his aged father's hand, he said with much earnestness, 'Stand up for Jesus, father; stand up for Jesus; and tell my brethren of the ministry, wherever you meet them, to stand up for Jesus.'" Thus he died on Monday, between one and two o'clock, surrounded by his family, with his intellect unclouded and his faith in the happy change that was awaiting him bright and clear and earnest.

The Rev. George Duffield, Jr., then pastor of Temple Presbyterian Church, Philadelphia, heard the account of his friend's passing at a memorial service at Jayne's Hall. He said, "Tyng was one of the noblest, bravest and manliest men I have ever met." The following Sunday morning he preached to his people from Ephesians 6:14, "Stand, therefore, having your loins girt about with truth." For his conclusion, he read an original poem of six stanzas, which, he explained, had been inspired by the dying words of his co-worker. The poem began:

> Stand up, stand up for Jesus, Ye soldiers of the cross;
> Lift high His royal banner, It must not suffer loss.
> From victory unto victory, His army shall He lead,
> Till every foe is vanquished, And Christ is Lord indeed.

The editor of a Hymnal, needing a new hymn for his book, joined these thrilling stanzas with a tune that George Webb had written for a poem, " 'Tis Dawn, the Lark Is Singing," for a show on board ship somewhere in the mid-Atlantic. The result is that in death, Dudley Atkins Tyng preached more widely and more successfully than ever he did in life. "Stand Up, Stand Up for Jesus" has inspired untold millions to nobler Christian living during its first century, and doubtless will continue its ministry even more effectively as its second century approaches.

44.

THE CHURCH IN THE WILDWOOD

When the building of a Church inspires the writing of a hymn, that isn't news; but when the writing of a song inspires the building of a Church, that's another story.

The Congregational Church in the agricultural hamlet of Bradford, Iowa, was organized November 4, 1855. For a meeting place the small congregation had used successively a store, several homes, an abandoned schoolhouse and even a lawyer's office. The financial panic that swept the country the following year made their situation even worse. Many of the faithful gave up their dreams of a Church building and resigned themselves to meeting here and there, wherever a large room was made available.

Then one June afternoon, William Savage Pitts, a twenty-seven-year-old student from Rush Medical School, made the 80-mile trip from McGregor, Iowa, to Bradford by stagecoach. During his brief stay he met the preacher of the local Church and learned of the people's desperate need for a new building all their own.

One afternoon he walked with a group of friends to the summit of a hill beyond the village. From the heights he could see much of surrounding Chickasaw County and the beauty of the Cedar River Valley. As they were visiting, the young student pointed to a grove of trees in the valley below and said, "If I were building a Church, I would build it down there in the lovely little vale, and I'd call it 'The Church in the Vale.' "

"What color would you paint it?" someone asked.

Pitts replied, "Schoolhouses are painted red, and dream cottages for young lovers are always white. But since the folks don't have much money, and brown paint is the cheapest, I'd paint it brown."

To which his friend quickly added, "And call it, 'The Little Brown Church in the Vale'!"

Pitts answered, "Yes; and we'll even write a song about it to popularize the new Church."

When the young medical student resumed his studies in the fall, he could not forget his vision of a "little brown Church in the vale." It haunted him until he studied the hymnals to discover what others had written about the Church. Most of the hymns were majestic and inspiring, while the song he wanted to write about his "dream Church" needed the lilt of a Stephen Foster melody, and the simplicity of the popular folk songs.

"The song should fit the Church," he thought. One night the inspiration came, and Pitts wrote his lines down as he hummed the music which now is familiar to millions. His song began:

> There's a Church in the valley by the wildwood,
> No lovelier place in the dale;
> No spot is so dear to my childhood,
> As the little brown Church in the vale.

Two years after Pitts visited Bradford, and selected "the ideal spot for a new Church," the Rev. John K. Nutting was called to be the pastor of Bradford Congregational Church. He heard of the young physician who had envisioned a Church in the vale and inspired his congregation to make Pitts' dream a reality. Members volunteered to do most of the work themselves. Friends back east sent enough money to have the rough lumber dressed and finished. The people of Bradford, in New England, sent a new bell to the children of their neighbors who had gone out years before to name their midwestern town after their distant home community.

Meanwhile, Dr. Pitts had fallen in love with that section of Iowa, and, following the completion of his medical studies, had settled in Fredericksburg, just twenty miles from Bradford. In addition to his work as a doctor, he conducted singing schools as his hobby. Soon after he introduced his song in one of the local singing schools, the "Little Brown Church in the Vale" was completed and dedicated on December 29, 1864.

As the fame of the song grew, people came from miles around

to worship in the Church that had been inspired by the song. Dr. Pitts lived and labored in Iowa for 44 years. When railroads came through that section of the state, the trains for Chickasaw County ran through the town of Nashua, two miles from Bradford. Soon most of the townspeople moved to Nashua to be near the railroad and Bradford became almost a "deserted village."

But, through the years, thousands have visited the little brown Church in the vale, remembering the talented young physician who immortalized the Church in his popular gospel song.

45.

THE NINETY AND NINE

If an "inner voice" had not prompted Ira D. Sankey to compose an impromptu tune for a new poem on the spur of the moment, one of the most popular gospel songs would never have been born. In fact, Sankey had never seen the words his music made world-famous until a couple of days before he spontaneously picked out the tune as he sat at his portable organ before several thousand people at Free Assembly Hall, Edinburgh, Scotland, one noonday in 1874.

He and Dwight L. Moody were enroute from Glasgow to Edinburgh, after a strenuous four months of meetings in the former city, to hold a three-day campaign there at the urgent invitation of the Ministerial Association. Just before boarding the train, Sankey bought a weekly newspaper for one penny, little dreaming that it would be the best penny he ever spent. Looking through the paper for some news of his homeland, he found nothing American but a sermon by Henry Ward Beecher. In disgust, he threw the paper down, only to pick it up a while later to pass the time by reading the advertisements. Then it was that he discovered a little piece of poetry in a corner of one column that he had carelessly overlooked during his first reading. He read it, liked it, and decided at once that it would make an effective song if someone set it to music. When he read it to Mr. Moody, the famous lay-preacher nodded a polite reply, as he was too busily engrossed in reading some letters from his family in the United States to hear a word his equally famous song-leader had read. Anyway, Sankey clipped the poem and put it in his musical scrapbook.

At the noonday service the second day of the special series in Edinburgh, Moody preached on "The Good Shepherd." Following his message, Dr. Horatius Bonar, author of "I Heard the Voice of Jesus Say" and other popular hymns, said a few words, thrilling the audience with his eloquence. When he sat down, Moody turned to his song-leader and asked, "Have you a solo appropriate for this subject with which to close the service?"

Sankey confessed that he had absolutely nothing in mind. It was precisely at this moment that the "inner voice" said, "Sankey, sing the hymn you found on the train." He replied, "That is impossible; there is no music for it." But the "voice" insisted. Sankey protested, "I can possibly bluff my way through the first stanza, but what of the rest?" To which the "voice" replied, "You take care of the first and leave the rest to me."

As calmly as if he had sung it a thousand times, he placed the little piece of newspaper on the organ in front of him, lifted up his heart in a brief prayer, and laid his hands on the keyboard, striking a chord in A flat. Half-speaking and half-singing, he completed the first stanza:

There were ninety and nine that safely lay, In the shelter of the fold;
But one was out on the hills away, Far off from the gates of gold.
Away on the mountains, wild and bare, Away from the tender shepherd's care.

The vast congregation listened in a spirit of hushed expectancy as he sang the five stanzas of this magnificent new song. When the echoes from the final notes of the last line, "Rejoice, I have found my sheep," died away, Moody walked over to the organ and said, with tears in his eyes, "Where did you get that hymn?"

Sankey replied, "That is the hymn I read to you yesterday on the train."

While the song has not been altered in so much as a note from that day to this, "The Ninety and Nine" became the most famous tune Sankey ever composed, and the hymn is more popular today than it was when he first played it over three-quarters of a century ago.

46.

THE OLD RUGGED CROSS

The most popular gospel song of the twentieth century is not an old favorite at all. It is a new favorite, written and composed in 1913 by Rev. George Bennard. He was born at Youngstown, Ohio, and his parents moved to Albia, Iowa when he was a mere babe. A few years later they moved again, settling down for a few years in Lucas, Iowa, where young George was converted. When his father died during the youth's sixteenth year, he became the sole support of his mother and four sisters, so he was unable to secure the education he desired in preparation for the Christian ministry.

The successes of his later life are all the more remarkable because of the struggles that marked his youthful years. The family moved to Illinois some years later, where the young man married. He and his wife then took training and served for a while as officers in the Salvation Army, later uniting with the Methodist Church. Meantime musical friends had encouraged him to develop his talents and gave what assistance they could to make this possible.

During the early years of his ministry, he was "praying for a full understanding of the cross and its plan in Christianity." Consequently, he spent many hours in study, prayer and meditation until he could say, "I saw the Christ of the cross as if I were seeing John 3:16 leave the printed page, take form and act out the meaning of redemption." During these days the theme of what was to be his most successful song came to him. He wanted to do something with it right then and there but heeded an inner voice that said "Wait!" Revival campaigns in Michigan and New York prevented him from working on the song he wanted to write. But on his return to Michigan he passed through a "rather trying" experience, when he felt he knew the meaning of St. Paul's words, "the fellowship of his sufferings." Personal feelings coupled with revival successes made it possible for him to concentrate as never before, and the song seemed to come to him without too much effort on his part.

He was staying in the Methodist parsonage at Pokagon, Michigan, while engaged in a series of services in the Pokagon Church when he finally perfected his song and wrote down the words and music. He got his favorite guitar and asked his host and hostess, Rev. and Mrs. L. O. Bostwick, to listen to the stanzas as he played and sang them. In the parsonage kitchen, the host pastor and his wife were the first persons to hear "The Old Rugged Cross" as sung by the author-composer. When he had finished singing, the minister said to his guest, "God has given you a song that will never die. It has moved us as no other song ever has." They immediately asked him for the privilege of having plates cut and copies printed. On the night of June 7, 1913, Rev. Mr. Bennard introduced the song in the nearby Church, and then the five-voice choir sang it from his pencilled notes. Members of that historic choir were: Frank Virgil, Olive Marrs, Clara Virgil, William Thaldorf and Florence Jones, who was also the first organist to play the new song.

"Old Rugged Cross Day" is observed annually at this Church, and on a large stone nearby is carved the names of the original singers and the significance of the event.

The song became immediately popular. Introduced before a large convention in Chicago, its fame spread rapidly throughout the Christian world. The author sent a manuscript copy to Charles H. Gabriel, well-known composer of hymns, gospel songs and anthems and he returned it with this prophetic message, "You will hear from this song."

Paul had written "God forbid that I should glory save in the cross of our Lord Jesus Christ" (Galatians 6:14). John Bowring had been inspired by those words to write "In the Cross of Christ I Glory." Out of his own night of poverty, pain and prayer, George Bennard has sung of its power and his song continues to grow in popularity with every passing year.

A twelve-foot high wooden cross stands on a roadside near Reed City, Michigan, honoring the composer. On it are the words "Old Rugged Cross." A sign reminds passersby that this is the "Home of Living Author, Rev. Geo. Bennard."

The songs Paul and Silas sang at midnight caused an earthquake in the Philippian jail. The song that George Bennard sang out of the midnight of his own soul has caused many a spiritual earthquake in numerous hearts and brought countless thousands to the cross of which he had so eloquently sung.

47.

THE SWEET BY AND BY

This is the only successful gospel song to be written and composed in a drugstore. And it all came about because the druggist, thirty-one-year-old Samuel Fillmore Bennett, knew what kind of a prescription to write at the right time.

Bennett, a native of Erie County, New York, moved with his family to Elkhorn, Wisconsin during the middle of the nineteenth century, where he grew up to become the editor of a small-town newspaper, "The Independent." When the Civil War broke, he joined the army as a member of the Fortieth Wisconsin Volunteers, and remained in active service until the cessation of hostilities in 1865. Returning to Elkhorn, he opened up a drugstore, better known in his day as an apothecary shop.

Among his friends was Joseph P. Webster, a local musician of considerable ability, who had but recently toured the northern states with a quartet he himself had organized. The two men saw a great deal of each other during the next two years, collaborating on several songs, Bennett writing the words and Webster, a gifted violinist, composing the music. One morning in the late fall of 1867, a woman came into the drugstore and said to the proprietor, "Mr. Bennett, I met your friend Joe Webster down the street a few minutes ago. He looked as if he had lost his best friend. What's the matter?"

Bennett explained, "Well, you know how musicians are, up one day and down the next. But if you want to know how to cure him, I'll give you a prescription that hasn't failed yet."

"Is it written in Latin?" she asked.

"Oh, no," he explained. "It is written in plain everyday English. You see, Joe and I have been working on our new songbook for nearly two years. He writes music for my poems. Whenever he comes in here looking sad and gloomy and depressed, I just leave him alone for a while. If he doesn't snap out of it, I snap him out of it by writing a new poem for him to set to music. That's my special prescription. When he starts thinking up a new tune he forgets his troubles and worries and gets well in a jiffy." With that, she laughed, shook her head, picked up her packages and headed for home.

A little while later, Webster strolled into the drugstore and, without a word or glance of greeting, walked over to the stove to warm himself. Bennett waited a few minutes, and then said, "Morning, Joseph." When his friend did not respond, he added, "Well, you might as well get it off your chest now as later. What's the matter?"

Webster began pouring out all his accumulated aches and pains, disappointments and frustrations, as his friend listened quietly. Finally he concluded by saying, "Well, there's really no use getting excited, I guess. Everything will be all right in the by and by." Bennett interrupted, "What was that, Joe?" He replied, "I just said everything will be all right in the by and by." Leaving his friend standing by the stove, the druggist went to his desk, picked up a piece of paper and began writing. Two customers entered the store, but the owner refused to wait on them until he finished the work at hand, so they joined Webster about the stove. When one said to his companion, "Webster looks like he is down in the dumps," the musician said, "Don't worry about me, gentlemen. I was just telling Sam that everything will be all right in the by and by."

Bennett rose from the desk, picked up pen and ink from a nearby counter, and resumed his writing. A few moments later he handed the sheet of paper to Webster, and said, "Here is your prescription, Joe. I hope it works as well as it has in the past." Webster glanced at the paper and began reading aloud what his friend had written:

There's a land that is fairer than day, And by faith we can see
    it afar;
For the Father waits over the way, To prepare us a dwelling
    place there.
In the sweet by and by, We shall meet on that beautiful shore;
In the sweet by and by, We shall meet on that beautiful shore.

Picking up his fiddle, Webster began improvising a simple melody for the new stanzas. In a moment he was humming the tune for the chorus. "Hand me some paper," he said, "so I can jot down the notes before I forget them." He played the tune over two or three times, and then said to the three men, "We four make a good male quartet. Let's try the new song and see how it sounds." As they were singing, "The Sweet By and By" for the first time, R. R. Crosby, Mrs. Bennett's uncle, came into the store. When the men finished the second stanza, he said, "Gentlemen, I never heard that song before but it is immortal. I heard it as I came across the street and couldn't resist coming in and listening."

A few days later it was given to the public. Within two weeks, the song the druggist and violinist had written in less than half-an-hour was being sung by the boys and girls of Elkhorn. Published in Webster's and Bennett's book, "The Signet Ring," in 1868, it became the most popular and most successful song they ever wrote. While it was originally written on a piece of paper just five by seven inches in size, it was big enough to sing its way into the hearts of Christian people the world over.

48.

THIS IS MY FATHER'S WORLD

If Maltbie Babcock had taken some of his own advice, he probably would have lived longer than forty-three years. The son of a socially prominent Syracuse, N.Y. family, he succeeded in just about everything he attempted. During his college days, he excelled in athletics, dramatics, music and scholarship as well as in religious activities. Yet he was full of fun and glowed with a kind of holy joy wherever he went.

Following graduation from Auburn Theological Seminary, where, by virtue of his magnetic personality, deep faith in God and genuine optimism, he was an outstanding student and leader, he was ordained as a Presbyterian minister in his first pastorate in Lockport, New York. Often he would say to his people, "I am going out to see my Father's world." With that he would frequently run early in the morning or late at night to the brow of a nearby hill some two miles north of the city, to drink in the beauties of nature and commune with nature's God.

"This world is best for us," he would often say, "and we must make the most of it and do our best for it."

A few miles beyond the hill, from whose summit he could view the distant waters of Lake Ontario, was a deep ravine, where the pastor often found refuge from the duties of a busy pastorate. "It is something of a bird sanctuary," he would explain. "Sometimes as many as forty different varieties of birds can be found there, and I like to hear them raise their carols in praise to God." But the long walks and early morning hikes and the intimate communing with nature and God were soon to be put behind him but not before he wrote down his feelings in a sixteen-stanza poem which contained these lines:

This is my Father's world, And to my listening ears
All nature sings, and round me rings The music of the spheres.

When a call came from the prominent Brown Memorial Presbyterian Church, Baltimore, Maryland, the gifted young minister, not yet thirty years of age, left Lockport to assume the duties of the new pastorate. There he gave fourteen years of remarkable and magnificent service, not only to his Church but also to the students of Johns Hopkins and to the city at large. From his contagiously radiant personality large numbers and varieties of people drew spiritual strength. In 1899 he was called to succeed Henry van Dyke at the Brick Presbyterian Church in New York City. Although his people and city were loath to give him up, he felt that the opportunities in New York were too great to turn down.

"I feel that I can be of greater service in the metropolitan pulpit than here in Baltimore," he said, explaining why he accepted the call to New York.

But in his new parish he found fewer hours for communing with nature at the very time when he needed more. The pressures of caring for larger and larger congregations, coupled with the duties of administering the program of a growing Church, and ministering to the city at the same time, became more and more burdensome. While he took advantage of every opportunity to "get out into the fields with God," somehow they became fewer and farther between. It was then that the broad-shouldered, steel-muscled clergyman braced himself for the task before him, and penned these autobiographical lines:

Be strong! We are not here to play, to dream, to drift,
We have hard work to do and loads to lift;
Shun not the struggle. Face it. 'Tis God's gift. Be strong!

After eighteen months, his congregation gave him a trip to the Holy Land, hoping he could recuperate his powers during the ocean voyage and a visit to the land marked by the footsteps of the Lord. But on that trip, at the age of forty-three, at the very height of his influence and power, Maltbie Davenport Babcock died, under rather mysterious circumstances, in Naples, Italy, May 18, 1901.

Maybe he erred in his poem "Be strong!" because we *are* here to play, to dream and to drift, as much as to plan, to dare and to direct. The holiness of play is as sacred as the holiness of prayer. Had he taken the time to get out into nature more often, she would have worked her therapeutic magic on his mind as well as his heart and body, and he could have given many more years of useful service to the Kingdom of God.

Be that as it may, his wife gathered many of his poems, sermons and addresses together and published them the year of his death, under the title "Thoughts for Everyday Living," and it was in this volume that his two finest hymns were published for the first time.

49.

WHAT A FRIEND WE HAVE IN JESUS

Tragedy haunted the footsteps of Joseph Scriven with dogged persistence. Following his graduation from the University of Dublin, Ireland, with a Bachelor of Arts degree, in 1842, his twenty-third year, he fled his native Irish shores after the tragic drowning of his fiancee on the evening prior to their scheduled marriage. But he found little solace in flight, although he put thousands of miles between himself and the familiar sights and smells of Dublin.

Eventually, he arrived at Port Hope on the northern shore of Lake Ontario in the Canadian province from which the lake takes its name. But even there happiness was to be denied him. Ten miles north of the lakeshore town was a small settlement named Bewdley, on the shores of beautiful Rice Lake. Several miles beyond was the Pengelley estate where Scriven lived for many years as private tutor for the children of the family.

Some years later he began dividing his time between the Pengelley home and that of Mr. James Sackville in Bewdley; it was in a guest-room in the Sackville home that he was inspired to write the poem with which his name is forever linked. Late one night in 1855, weighted down with loneliness and overcome with despondency and sadness, he poured out his heart to God, begging for relief from his burden and promising to serve Him faithfully if only his prayer were answered. God heard and answered, and Joseph Scriven felt the burden miraculously lifted from his heart.

In his new-found joy he hurriedly dashed off a very simple poem of several stanzas in which he described his struggle and victory. The poem, entitled "Pray without Ceasing," began with these lines:

What a friend we have in Jesus, All our sins and griefs to bear;
What a privilege to carry Everything to God in prayer.
O what peace we often forfeit, O what needless pain we bear,
All because we do not carry Everything to God in prayer.

Falling in love for the second time, he became engaged to
Miss Eliza Catherine Roche, only daughter of Lieut. Andrew
Roche of the Royal Navy. However, she contracted tubercu-
losis and died in 1860, before their wedding could take place.

Following two such tragic blows, he gave himself more dili-
gently to religious and philanthropic work, becoming associated
with the Plymouth Brethren group, and serving them as a lay-
preacher for many years. In addition, he preached for a while in
the Bailieboro Baptist Church nearby. But he endeared himself
to the people in and around Bewdley because of his Christ-like
life, and his habit of giving away all his private income to the
poor whom he considered in more urgent need than himself.
In later years he was described as "a man of short stature, with
iron-gray hair, close-cropped beard, and light blue eyes that
sparkled when he talked." Someone else said "he had the face of
an angel" while another who knew him well spoke of his habit of
"preaching to everyone about the love of Jesus" as well as the
peculiarities that marked his declining years.

When his body was worn with toil and his mind wearied with
disappointment, Mr. Sackville took him into his home once more,
and it was there, in 1886, that Mr. Scriven spent the last days of
his life. In the same house in which he had written his poem
thirty-one years earlier, his host discovered it in the poet's scrapbook during the author's last and fatal illness. Scriven explained,
"The Lord and I did it between us."

Sackville made a copy for himself and another to send to a
religious journal where it was published for the first time.
Shortly thereafter, Scriven died. In his delirium he staggered
from his bedroom and stumbled, exhausted, into a little creek
about a hundred yards from the house, drowning in less than
six inches of water. His friends said, "He died on his knees, in
the attitude of prayer."

Although three monuments were erected to his memory in

and around Bewdley in 1919, the one-hundredth anniversary of his birth, his poem, set to music by C. C. Converse, had long since been enshrined in the hearts of Christians the world over, and has found a permanent place in the hymnody of the Church universal.

50.

WHEN I SURVEY THE WONDROUS CROSS

Some verses that pass for hymns are such cheap doggerel that they can hardly be called poems at all. When Church-goers in England in 1692 were subjected to such drivel in their public praise of God, few complained or protested; criticism of the Church was regarded as criticism of the State, since the Government supported the Established Church. And it was almost unthinkable that anyone in his right mind would speak of the Crown in such a flagrantly unbecoming manner.

But that didn't faze eighteen-year-old Isaac Watts. He openly ridiculed such stanzas as this:

Ye monsters of the bubbling deep, Your Maker's praise spout
    out;
Up from the sands ye coddlings peep, And wag your tails about.

In fact, he had so much to say about "these ugly hymns" that his disapproval soon incurred his father's displeasure.

"Isaac," the stern, austere Deacon said, "if you cannot be reverent, you can at least keep your mouth shut about things which do not concern you."

When Isaac and his brother, Enoch, explained that they were not only criticizing the hymns of the day but also were hoping someday to prepare their own hymnal to offer in its place, the elder Watts laughed and said sarcastically, "That old hymnal was good enough for your grandfather, and your father, so I reckon it will have to be good enough for you!"

Undismayed, the young men insisted upon a fair hearing from their sire, only to have him reply, caustically, "If you don't like our hymns, then let me hear one you have written which is better."

Isaac immediately leaped to his feet and said, "Father, I *have* one which is better. Will you listen to it?"

The older man looked up in surprise, paused, and then said, "Well, read it!"

Picking up a sheet of paper, the young English lad read:

Behold the glories of the Lamb, Amidst His Father's throne;
Prepare new honors for His Name, And songs before unknown!

When he finished reading the five stanzas of his first hymn, Deacon Watts rose, put his arms around him, apologized for his hasty words and asked for a copy of the new hymn. It was sung the following Sunday morning, and was so well received by the congregation that young Isaac was requested to prepare new hymns for succeeding Sundays. He complied with this unusual request for the next two-hundred-twenty-two weeks.

In 1712, he was invited to recuperate from a serious breakdown in the home of a former Lord Mayor of London, Sir Thomas, and Lady Abney. Although he planned to remain there but three weeks, Sir Thomas invited him to stay indefinitely as post Chaplain, a position he filled for thirty-six years. Lady Abney said of his long stay, "It seems the shortest visit a friend ever paid a friend."

During his residence there, Dr. Watts wrote more volumes of hymns, and almost single-handedly changed the congregational singing habits of English-speaking Christendom. From his pen came these perennial favorites, "Alas! And Did My Saviour Bleed," "Jesus Shall Reign," and the hymn which is generally regarded as the most perfect ever written in our tongue:

When I survey the wondrous cross, On which the Prince of
  Glory died;
My richest gain I count but loss, And pour contempt on all my
  pride.

Although he died in 1748 at the age of seventy-five, this line from the inscription on a stone monument to his honor which stands in a beautiful suburban London cemetery, attests to his greatness, "Ages unborn will make his songs The joy and labor of their tongues."

INDEX

(Numbers refer to chapters rather than pages)